N°5

CHANEL
CHANEL
CHANEL
CHANEL

CHANEL
CHANEL
CHANEL

Nº 5
CHANEL
PARIS

N° 5
CHANEL
PARIS

pp. 2–3:
Gabrielle Chanel, photographed by Horst P. Horst, 1937.
pp. 4–5:
Perfume bottles in the windows of the Chanel boutique at 31 rue Cambon, Paris, 1920s.
pp. 6–7:
Box packaging for N°5 perfume (left), 1924; bottle for N°5 perfume, 1924 (right).

N°5

ANATOMY OF A MYTH

PAULINE DREYFUS

CONTENTS

1

THE HEIGHT OF MODERNITY

AS 1920 CAME TO A CLOSE, GABRIELLE CHANEL CELEBRATED NEW YEAR'S EVE IN HER COUTURE HOUSE AT 31 RUE CAMBON. Despite her undeniable professional success, her heart was broken. A year earlier, Boy Capel, the great love of her life, had been killed in a road accident. The designer drowned her sorrows in her work. In her mourning she even had the walls of her bedroom in Garches painted black. To help clear her head, her great friend Misia Sert, the flamboyant redhead whom the press nicknamed 'the Queen of Paris', took the grieving Gabrielle to Italy. Venice was a shock to her system. Gabrielle would never forget this trip, taken in the company of Misia's third husband, the artist José María Sert, a large and talkative man who introduced Gabrielle to art in general and to painting in particular. She also met or renewed her acquaintance with members of the Russian diaspora, in mourning for the empire of the tsars, including the art patron Sergei Diaghilev, whose Ballets Russes were already the talk of Paris. These things brought light into Gabrielle's dark chamber of grief.

Previous page: Gabrielle Chanel, 1929.

From the moment they had first met at the home of the actress Cécile Sorel, Misia and Gabrielle had been bound by friendship. It was to this bosom friend that the designer owed not only her education in art but also her instruction in social mores, at a time when members of high society did not mingle with tradespeople. Misia had opened the closed doors of an aristocratic world to Gabrielle, where nobody would previously have dreamed of inviting a seamstress, even a high-fashion one. Gabrielle Chanel – who hated being in debt, or even feeling that way – therefore asked the considerate and generous Misia to invite her friends *chez Chanel* for New Year's Eve. The buffet was laid out in the fitting rooms. The setting was suitably offbeat and the hostess already renowned: it was an evening that nobody would dare to miss. Some thirty guests came to share this unforgettable New Year's Eve. To welcome them, Gabrielle dressed in her uniform of choice: a black velvet gown and three rows of pearls.

The guest list was a dream: all the stars of the artistic avant-garde were there, every one of them already beginning to shape the century. There was Jean Cocteau, who had been rocketed to fame by the provocative production of his ballet *Parade* in 1917 and trailing Paris's greatest talents in his stylish wake. He arrived in the company of a promising young poet, Raymond Radiguet, who was writing an inflammatory novel about the war, *Le Diable au corps*. There was also the writer Paul Morand, who was soon to publish *Tendres stocks*, a collection of nervy short stories whose dry style made the wandering sentences of his friend Marcel Proust look outdated; composer Erik Satie, spiritual father of Cocteau's Group of Six, and a friend of

Georges Braque and the Dada group; dancer Serge Lifar, star of Diaghilev's controversial Ballets Russes; Pablo Picasso, who had shaken up the perspectives inherited from Renaissance art with his Cubist paintings; composer Darius Milhaud, who had imported a craze for South American music from Brazil; composer Georges Auric, whose foxtrots for piano and orchestra disconcerted staid music-lovers; poet Blaise Cendrars, who was about to publish *Anthologie nègre*; plus the painter André Dunoyer de Segonzac and the diplomat Philippe Berthelot, who were always around when something interesting was going on. It was a glittering evening that presaged a new era.

The poet Guillaume Apollinaire had died two years earlier from the Spanish flu, but not before he had coined a new word: Surrealism. Gabrielle Chanel's guests knew his verses by heart, and without a second thought they stepped into the breach that the poet had opened, as if reciting en masse the opening line from his poetry collection *Alcools* of 1913: 'In the end you are weary of this ancient world.' The thing they all had in common with the lady of the house was that they had all, in their own ways, stirred up controversy.

They say you only meet people whom you already like. Even without Misia's adept social skills, Gabrielle Chanel and the great artists of her time would surely have found each other anyway. From the very start, she displayed highly distinctive tastes. She financed a revival of Diaghilev's *Rite of Spring*, having sadly missed its pre-war premiere – a memorable evening whose aftershocks could still be felt in Paris. Moreover, its composer, Igor Stravinsky, had also been staying at her home since autumn 1920. Through Misia, she got to know Pierre Reverdy, a poet who was close to the Cubists and who founded the short-lived literary review *Nord-Sud* and brought public recognition to poets and writers such as Max Jacob, André Breton, Louis Aragon and Tristan Tzara. In 1918, Gabrielle had started designing theatre costumes. She was shortly to dress the actors in Cocteau's *Antigone*.

Gabrielle Chanel was just like the artists who arrived at the rue Cambon solely on the recommendation of Misia, who was ever alert to the slightest ripple of new talent or modernity: 'in certain dim lights, she performs her useful and kindly act like a glow-worm in the dark'.[1] In her own field – fashion – Gabrielle, too, was the originator of an aesthetic revolution.

It was no surprise that an immediate bond formed between Gabrielle Chanel and those in the modernist vanguard. This child of a travelling salesman, this orphan girl entrusted to the nuns of the Abbaye d'Aubazine and thrown back into secular life due to a lack of religious vocation, this bedroom seamstress who tried to better herself by singing in the cafés of Moulins – which did not bring her fame but did give her the lifelong and world-famous nickname of 'Coco' – had the insatiable curiosity of the self-taught.

N°5, which was to see the light of day less than five months later, was born out of this fertile melting pot.

1

2

3

4

5

1. The writer Blaise Cendrars, *c.* 1924–25.
2. Jean Cocteau, Pablo Picasso, Igor Stravinsky and Olga Picasso, Juan-les-Pins, 1925.
3. Jean Cocteau (seated at the piano) with the Group of Six: (from left to right) Darius Milhaud, a drawing representing Georges Auric, Arthur Honegger, Germaine Tailleferre, Francis Poulenc and Louis Durey.
4. The composer Erik Satie, 1910s.
5. The pianist and art patron Misia Sert, *c.* 1920–25.

6

7

8

9

6. The writer Paul Morand, 1910.
7. Gabrielle Chanel, 1920.
8. The writer Raymond Radiguet.
9. The Russian dancer and choreographer Serge Lifar, *c.* 1927.

BOY CAPEL

(1881–1919)

1

Arthur Capel, or Boy, as everyone called him, first met Gabrielle Chanel in 1907 through her then-lover Étienne Balsan. Some said that this handsome young man, with his dark complexion and thick hair, was the illegitimate son of one of the Péreire brothers, a family of bankers. A passionate polo player, he made his fortune exporting coal from north-east England. He was soon enchanted by this young woman who was the very antithesis of the buxom blonde beauties of the Belle Époque.

When Gabrielle decided to open a boutique selling hats, Boy was the only one who supported her. It was thanks to him that in late 1910 she set up shop at 21 rue Cambon. 'She is on her own, she gets bored, and this irritates me. It's not difficult to get two hearts to beat in time, but it's hard to synchronize two watches,' said Boy to the writer Élisabeth de Gramont.[1] A good incentive, but Gabrielle and Boy also shared a love of business and risk.

Together they moved into an apartment on the avenue Gabriel, filled with the Coromandel lacquer screens that they both loved. Boy noticed how shortsighted Gabrielle was and bought her glasses, explaining that the condition had been fortunate in her case because it had allowed her to cultivate her sense of touch: 'You have the highly developed hands of a shortsighted person. When you're testing or

1. Gabrielle Chanel, Étienne Balsan and Arthur 'Boy' Capel, *c.* 1912.
2. Boy Capel reading in his apartment, *c.* 1911.

2

1

examining a fabric, you look like a sommelier tasting wine.'[II] In 1916, having become successful, she was in a position to pay him back for his generosity. 'I thought I'd given you a plaything; I gave you freedom,'[III] he said in a melancholy tone.

Boy was Gabrielle's great love, though – concerned about respectability and harbouring political ambitions – he never proposed to her and instead married into British high society at the end of the First World War. As something of a Pygmalion figure, he shared his literary interests with Gabrielle and introduced her to the dancer Isadora Duncan. Gabrielle took inspiration from her lover's polo jerseys for some of her first creations, blurring the distinction between masculine and feminine clothes. Boy's friends flocked to Gabrielle's boutique, which opened in 1912 in Deauville; the caricaturist Sem even drew Boy as a centaur in a polo outfit, carrying off a woman who was clearly meant to be Gabrielle. Everyone knew that Chanel's backer was also her lover. For Gabrielle, it was wonderful publicity.

On 22 December 1919, Boy Capel died in a car crash on the road to Cannes. At the time of his death, he had been reading the latest winner of the Prix Goncourt, *À l'ombre des jeunes filles en fleurs* (*In the Shadow of Young Girls in Flower*, the second volume of *In Search of Lost Time*) by Marcel Proust. Gabrielle Chanel rushed south from Paris, but arrived too late for the funeral. Although Boy was married to someone else, Gabrielle was the one who felt widowed.

1. Gabrielle Chanel with Boy Capel and Constant Say (seen from rear) on the beach at Saint-Jean-de-Luz, 1917.
2. Gabrielle Chanel on horseback, with Boy Capel, *c.* 1910.

2

1

2

3

1. A gathering outside the Chanel boutique in Deauville: Gabrielle Chanel stands in the doorway, Boy Capel is sitting on her right, and Étienne Balsan is on the far left, 1913.
2. Photograph of Gabrielle Chanel wearing one of her own hat designs, published in the theatre magazine *Comœdia Illustré*, 1 October 1910.
3. Gabrielle Chanel and her aunt Adrienne, in front of the Chanel boutique in Deauville, *c.* 1913.

4

5

4. Gabrielle Chanel in Étretat, *c.* 1913.
5. Illustration from article on the Maison Chanel, *Vogue*, October 1921.

MISIA SERT

(1872–1950)

1

Born Misia Godebska in St Petersburg, she grew up in Belgium, then in France. Her father was a mainstay of the literary and artistic circles of Paris. At the age of twenty-one, she married Thadée Natanson, who had just founded *La Revue blanche*, a literary journal that promoted new writers. Famed for her beauty, Misia became a favourite model of artists Pierre Bonnard and Édouard Vuillard. *La Revue blanche* hit trouble after losing many readers as a result of its position on the Dreyfus case. In 1900, the press magnate Alfred Edwards offered to clear Natanson's debts on the condition that he divorced Misia. After the deal was done, Edwards married Misia in 1905 and gave her the gift of a yacht, which welcomed regular guests including the artist Auguste Renoir, the actress Réjane and the composer Maurice Ravel. Misia became so renowned that journalists nicknamed her 'the Queen of Paris'.

In 1908, she fell in love at first sight with a Spanish painter, José María Sert. He introduced her to Sergei Diaghilev, who got her involved with the creation of the Ballets Russes. Now a patron, she financed the ballet *Parade*, staged by Jean Cocteau at the Théâtre du Châtelet in 1917. Most of all, she loved to watch over and encourage

1, 2. Misia Sert in Cannes, photographed by the painter Édouard Vuillard, *c.* 1901.

2

1

new talents. When a young poet and admirer of Mallarmé, Pierre Reverdy, founded the journal *Nord-Sud* to promote Cubism, Surrealism and Dada, she bought a large number of copies and sent a monthly cheque to its director.

It was at a dinner hosted by the actress Cécile Sorel in 1917 that Misia first met Gabrielle Chanel. They soon became inseparable. With her husband's help, Misia educated Gabrielle in the ways of society and the art world. 'After having honed her taste and her eye, she turned the quiet provincial milliner into the tireless Chanel of the rue Cambon,' recorded Claude Arnaud, Cocteau's biographer.[IV] In turn, Gabrielle, whose business was booming, offered financial aid to artists discovered by Misia, including the young Raymond Radiguet. When Sert left Misia, she fell ill and was looked after by Gabrielle. They were together on the Duke of Westminster's yacht in 1929 when a telegram arrived with the news that Diaghilev was dying in Venice; they rushed to his bedside, and subsequently organized his funeral.

Distraught over her separation, Misia sought refuge in morphine and the addiction proved fatal. When she died in October 1950, Gabrielle prepared Misia's body for the funeral herself. Resting on a bier of white flowers, she was dressed all in white, with a satin sash across her chest, decorated with a simple rose. 'It was Chanel's last offering of peace and love,' their mutual friends declared.[V]

In 2015, Chanel released a perfume named Misia in her honour.

2

3

1. Woodcut print by Félix Vallotton showing Misia Sert at the piano, 1897.
2. Misia Natanson, the future Misia Sert, dressed up as a man, *c.* 1900.
3. Misia Sert wearing a Chanel gown for a party, the Bal des Ballons, held at the studio of José María Sert.

4

5

6

4. Misia Sert and Gabrielle Chanel (below) with Igor Stravinsky and José María Sert (above) at the Foire de Paris, 1920.
5. Pablo Picasso (second from right) sitting on the curtain he designed for the ballet *Parade*, Théâtre du Châtelet, Paris, 1917.
6. Gabrielle Chanel, José María Sert (standing behind), Misia Sert and Hélène Berthelot at the Lido beach in Venice, 1925.

1

2

3

4

1. Pablo Picasso, *Portrait of Pierre Reverdy*, ink on paper, 1921.
2. Pablo and Olga Picasso outside a theatre, *c.* 1917.
3. Sergei Diaghilev, impresario and founder of the Ballets Russes, 1916.
4. Scene from the ballet *The Rite of Spring*, with a score by Igor Stravinsky, Théâtre des Champs-Élysées, Paris, 1 January 1913.

5

6

A L'ATELIER

ANTIGONE

HÉMON (M. Allibert) CRÉON (M. Dullin) (M. Dullin)

ANTIGONE (Mlle Atanasiou) UN MESSAGER (M. Arnaud) ANTIGONE (Mlle Atanasiou) UN MESSAGER (M. Vital) Photos Gilbert-René.

7

5. Gabrielle Chanel photographed by Man Ray, 1930.
6. The composer Igor Stravinsky, *c.* 1920.
7. Page from the magazine *Le Théâtre* devoted to *Antigone*, the play by Jean Cocteau with sets by Pablo Picasso and costumes by Gabrielle Chanel, Théâtre de l'Atelier, Paris, January 1923.

JEAN COCTEAU

(1889–1963)

1

Paul Morand said of Jean Cocteau: 'He couldn't miss the train because he ran in front of it.'[VI] This brilliant poet, playwright and draughtsman was the multi-talented impresario of his age. Avant-garde artists gravitated around him, collaborating and helping each other. They called their friendship group the 'Mutual Admiration Society'. Cocteau met Gabrielle through Misia Sert, who like him was close to Diaghilev.

In 1922, the Théâtre de l'Atelier staged *Antigone*, in a free adaptation by Cocteau. The sets were by Picasso, the music by Arthur Honegger and the costumes by Chanel. Cocteau put her on the same level as his other two prestigious collaborators: 'I asked Mademoiselle Chanel to design the costumes, because she is the greatest couturière of our age, and I could not imagine the daughters of Oedipus being badly dressed.'[VII] It was the start of a long collaboration between the two, followed by *Le Train bleu*, *Orphée*, *Oedipe Roi* and then *Les Chevaliers de la Table ronde*, which Gabrielle was said to have financed. It seemed as if Cocteau could not envisage his characters being dressed in anything but Chanel.

1. Jean Cocteau, *c.* 1920.
2. Jean Cocteau, *c.* 1924.

2

1

2

3

Their collaboration shifted from artistic to commercial. Cocteau began to rewrite Gabrielle's press releases; he gave her advice on window displays for the rue Cambon and suggested designs for her jewelry range.

During this period, Cocteau was caught up in an unrequited passion for a young man who was just beginning his literary career. When Raymond Radiguet (nicknamed Monsieur Bébé – 'Mister Baby' – by the whole circle), was struck down by typhoid at the age of just twenty, it was Gabrielle whom Cocteau called for help. She had Radiguet hospitalized, but it was in vain. She took care of every detail and arranged his funeral at Saint-Honoré-d'Eylau. Unaware of this, his friends thanked the ever-present Misia.

Cocteau, nicknamed Le Veuf sur le Toit ('the widower on the roof', a play on the famous cabaret *Le Boeuf sur le Toit*) tried to throw himself into his work, but the opium he took to deal with his grief began to threaten his life. Once again, it was Gabrielle who paid for his stints in rehab. She was a discreet and exemplary patron, leading people to say: 'Literary young men fluttered around Coco like drunken butterflies. She gave them monthly stipends, which the publisher Bernard Grasset jokingly called "the Great Mademoiselle's pensions".'[VIII]

1. Jean Cocteau (sitting facing the camera) with the Group of Six, photographed by Man Ray: (from left to right) Francis Poulenc, Germaine Tailleferre, Louis Durey, Georges Auric (not present, drawn by Cocteau), Darius Milhaud and Arthur Honegger, 1931.
2. The writer Raymond Radiguet drawn by Jean Cocteau, early 1920s.
3. Génica Athanasiou in *Antigone*, wearing a costume by Gabrielle Chanel, photographed by Man Ray, 1922.

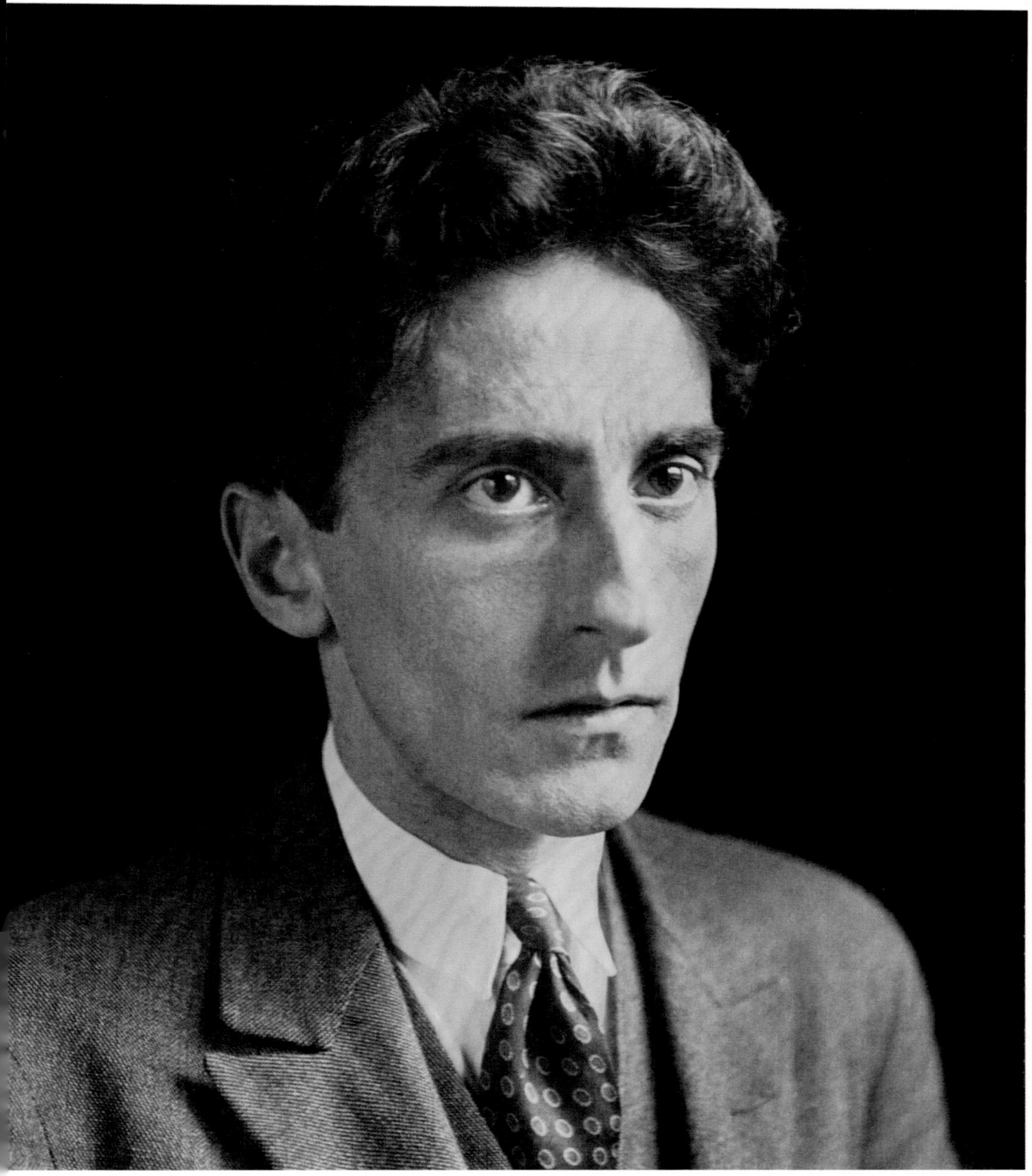

4

5

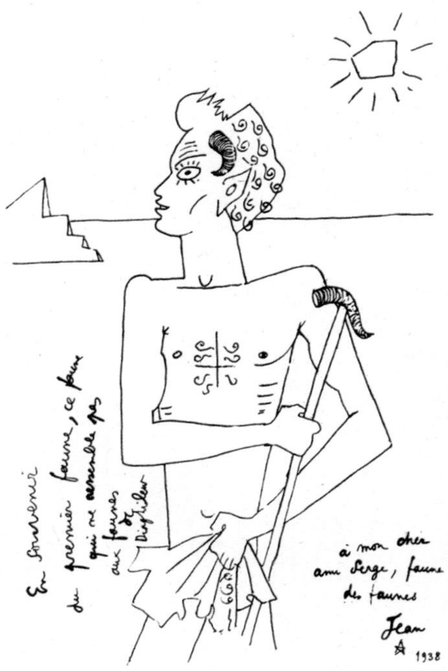

6

7

4. Jean Cocteau, 1923.
5. An image from *Antigone* by Jean Cocteau, published in *Vogue* Paris, February 1923.
6. Drawing by Jean Cocteau depicting Serge Lifar in the role of the faun in the ballet *L'Après-midi d'un faune*, set to music by Claude Debussy, 1938.
7. The Group of Six at the Eiffel Tower, 1921.

*

Before the war, Gabrielle had started making ladies' hats. Unlike the towering cake-like confections covered in flowers, feathers and velvet bows that weighed down the heads of fashionable ladies, the young milliner's hats were restrained, almost masculine, and yet strikingly chic. Paired with the new cropped hairstyles, they were elegance itself.

Her first clients attended the same horse races as she did. At her atelier-salon on the boulevard Malesherbes, customers from the world of racing were soon joined by a wider clientele. Her hats were followed by collections of clothes, with an emphasis on line, comfort and clarity. Now based in Deauville, in a boutique situated between the Hôtel Normandy and the casino, Gabrielle created an image of startling contrasts with her androgynously cut suits, open-necked shirts and round-toed shoes. When war broke out in early August 1914, it found her in this bustling resort.

Gabrielle Chanel began to make her first comfortable dresses for society ladies turned nurses. Her sailor shirts, cut loose so that they could be worn without a corset, became all the rage. She was firm in her belief that respecting nature did not have to mean a loss of femininity. These elegant but practical outfits reflected the mood of the times. Her garments brought a sense of freedom to women who were keen to break away from predetermined destinies. For clients who were beginning to emancipate themselves while the men were at the front, this active woman designed dresses with restrained lines, which did not emphasize either the waist or the hips, but revealed more of the ankles than ever before. Corsets were now nothing but a bad memory. Well before trousers came into fashion, she created beach pyjamas, a first step towards unisex style.

In 1915, Gabrielle continued the venture in Biarritz, where, thanks to a financial investment from Boy Capel, she opened not merely a boutique, but a real couture house. She bought in a supply of knitted jersey fabric from the firm Rodier, and the loose coats and monochrome jackets she made from it were quickly snapped up. This success provoked the fury of the couturier Paul Poiret, who commented that Gabrielle Chanel had invented 'poverty de luxe'[2] and that she had made women look like underfed telegraph clerks. His acerbic remarks did nothing to stem the popularity of this new fashion.

When Armistice was declared, there was no longer any question of returning to old habits. Forever unmarried, Gabrielle had no wish to be mistaken for one of the *demi-mondaines* who moved in the circles she frequented. The fanciful frills of the kept women and the flounces of the courtesans – which were nonetheless copied by society women – suddenly went out of style. Her androgynous silhouette was the embodiment of this new age. Like the works of the writers, artists and composers she mingled with, her art was rooted firmly in the rejection of old traditions. To this emancipated designer, elegance meant freedom of movement: 'I want women to be [...] free. Free to swing their arms and move quickly. In tune with the times.'[3] Within her own field, Gabrielle Chanel was truly 'the exterminating angel of 19th-century style', in the apt words of Paul Morand.[4] Her clothes made Worth look outdated, Paquin look faded and Poiret look ridiculous. The opening of her Paris couture house in 1918, on the rue Cambon, at the very epicentre of Parisian elegance, was a monument to her success.

1

2

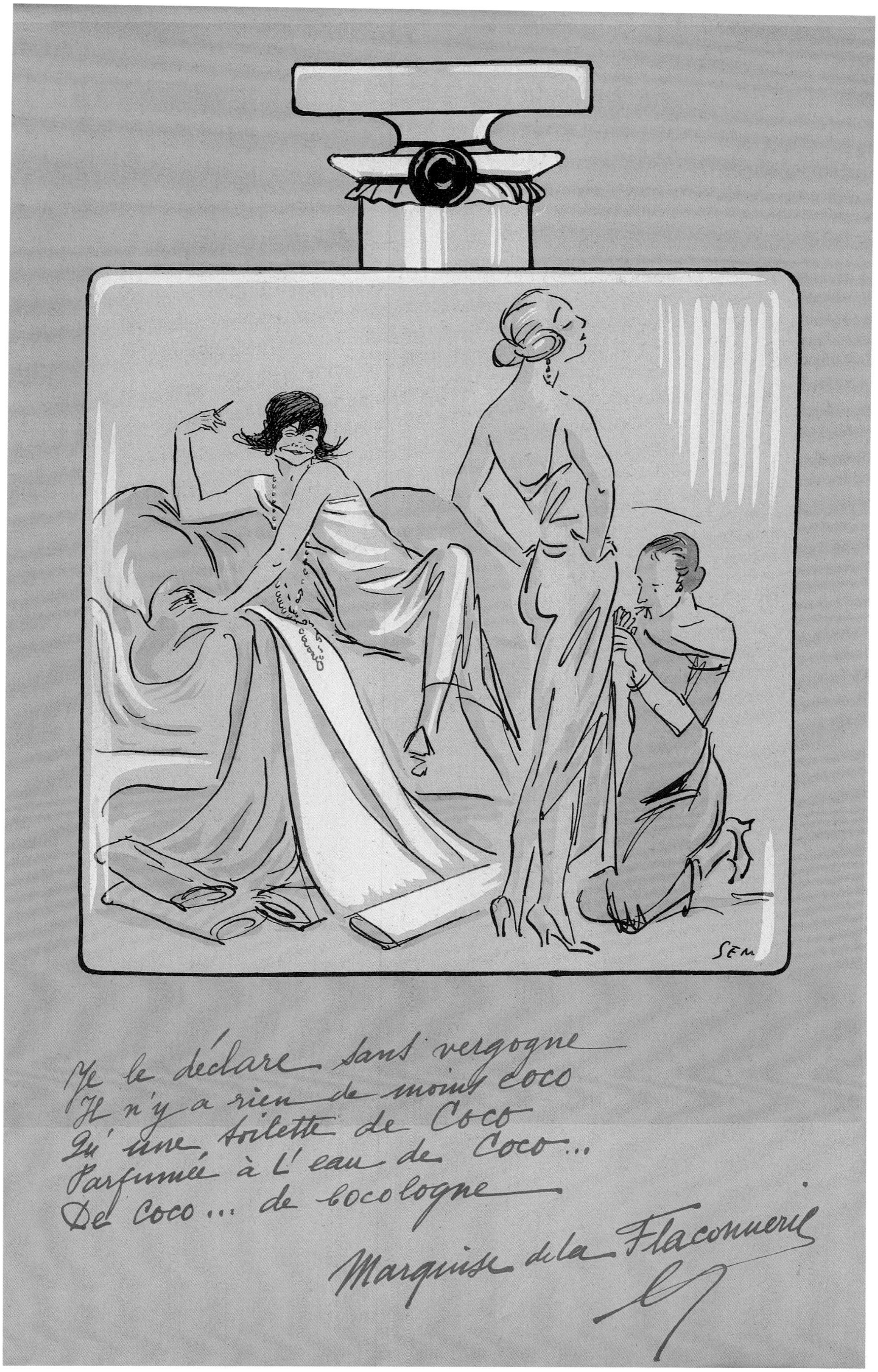

3

1. Caricature by Sem (Georges Goursat), depicting Gabrielle Chanel with Boy Capel, 1913.
2. The Chanel boutique in Biarritz, 1931.
3. 'Gabrielle Chanel or the Marquise of the Perfume Bottle', a caricature by Sem, 1923.

1er Janvier 9

DES NŒUDS DE TISSUS

DÉCORENT

TAILLES ET ENCOLURES

CHANEL

(A gauche) Le corsage partiellement découpé est un détail fréquemment répété par Chanel. L'ampleur est donnée à cette robe de satin noir par deux sections en forme incrustées dans le dos. Ceinture drapée et nouée

CHANEL

(Au-dessus) Les nœuds de tissu sont au nombre des garnitures les plus courantes. Ils ornent notamment cette robe de mousseline rouge, dont le corsage est fait de bandes diagonales, la jupe de deux volants superposés

2

1er Novembre

CHANEL

Cette robe en crêpe de Chine noir est le modèle type de Chanel : sobre, s'adaptant aisément aux circonstances, et d'une élégance impeccable dans sa simplicité. Pour toute ornementation, de fins plis lingerie groupés de manière à former une quadruple pointe dont les angles se rejoignent. La ligne n'offre nulle complication. Blousant devant et sur les côtés, le corsage est découpé dans le dos en boléro. La jupe enserre et moule légèrement les hanches, Encolure bateau ; manche longue et ajustée au bras

La Ligne Simple

1

1. A page devoted to Chanel evening gowns in *Vogue* Paris, January 1927.
2. 'The Simple Line', a page devoted to Chanel designs in *Vogue* Paris, November 1926.
3. Gabrielle Chanel photographed by Madame d'Ora, 1923.

3

2

FROM FASHION TO FRAGRANCE

IN JULY 1919, ENCOURAGED BY MISIA, GABRIELLE BEGAN TO DABBLE IN SKINCARE, INCLUDING AN EAU CHANEL INSPIRED, SO SHE SAID, BY A RECIPE FROM THE PERFUMER TO CATHERINE DE' MEDICI. She chose an austere, almost pharmaceutical bottle, as befitting her tastes. Eau Chanel sold well. Surprised and delighted, Gabrielle listened to Misia's suggestion that she should go further and create a perfume. The advice was sound: since Gabrielle Chanel wanted to dress a woman from head to toe, the effect would not be complete until she came up with a perfume that could work the same magic. Previously the only designer to combine the fashion business with perfumery had been Paul Poiret, with his Les Parfums de Rosine in 1911. However, he had made the serious mistake of naming the venture after his daughter rather than himself, thus failing to capitalize on the fame of his own brand. Gabrielle learned a lesson from this.

Nonetheless, the couturière prevaricated. She did not share Misia's enthusiasm, since she harboured a lasting prejudice against women who wore too much perfume, whom she suspected of trying to hide nasty odours. How often, in her younger years, had she encountered coquettes who doused themselves in heavy perfumes, in an era when hygiene was often questionable and bathing rare? The scents she liked were those that evoked cleanliness and good health. Later in her life,

Previous page: Gabrielle Chanel, 1936.

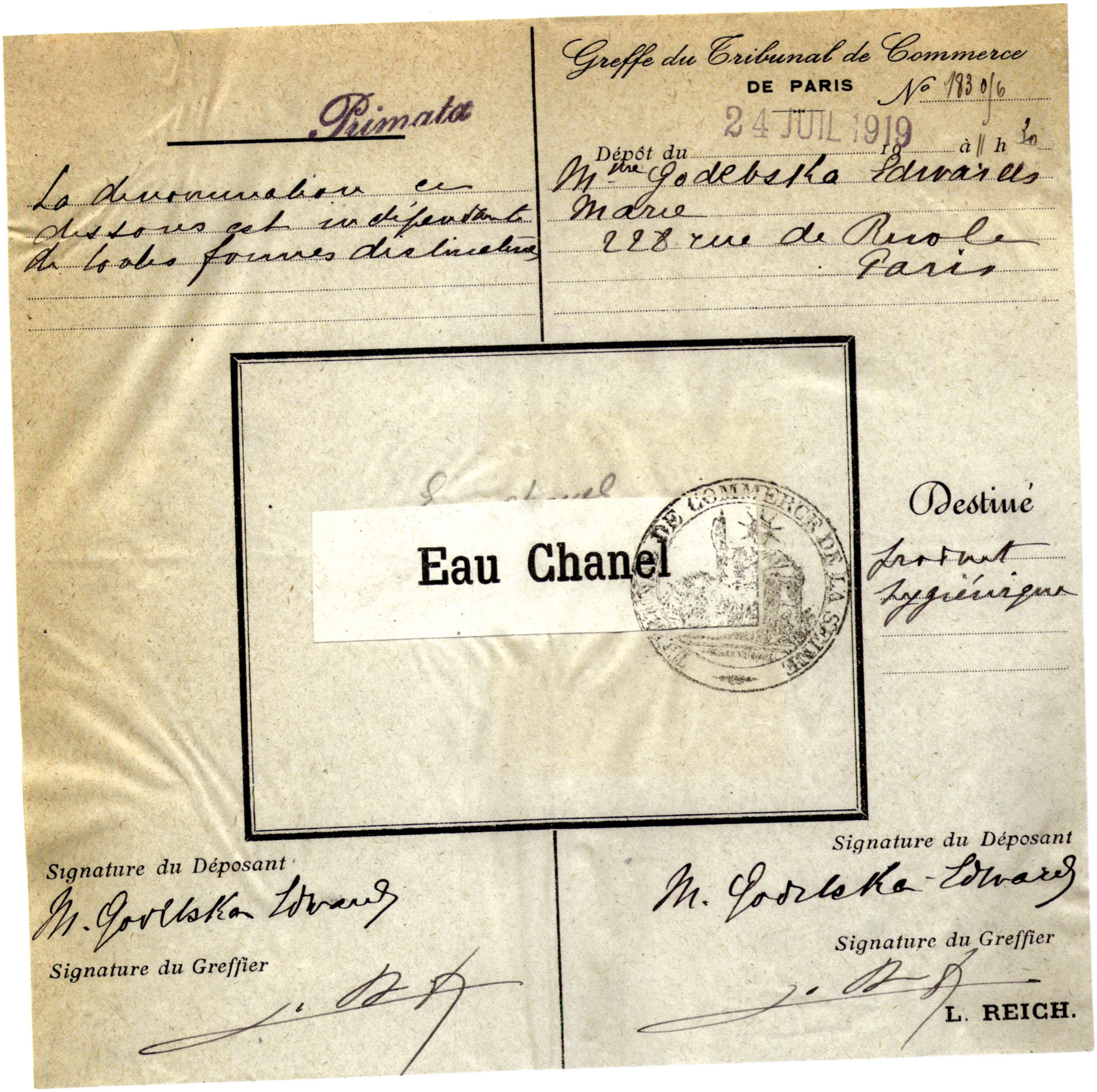
Greffe du Tribunal de Commerce
DE PARIS N° 183 0/6
24 JUIL 1919
Dépôt du 19 à 11 h 30
Mme Godebska Edwards
Marie
228 rue de Rivoli
Paris

Eau Chanel

TRIBUNAL DE COMMERCE DE LA SEINE

Destiné
produit
hygiénique

Signature du Déposant
M. Godebska Edwards

Signature du Greffier

L. REICH.

Trademark registration for Eau Chanel dated 24 July 1919, bearing the signature of Misia Godebska Edwards (the future Misia Sert).

she spoke of Émilienne d'Alençon, a courtesan who had been involved with her former lover Étienne Balsan, saying only that she 'smelled clean'.[5]

'I am a couturière, not a perfumer, and I disapprove of everything that perfumers do,' she said.[6] Perhaps her widening circle of acquaintances had made her change her mind.

Goodbye 1920, hello 1921. The new year was bursting with promise; the past was buried for good. The war and its parade of horrors were far away. Once again, merriment was allowed. Paris rediscovered its love of celebration, charm and imagination. Art boomed on both banks of the river; a new world was being celebrated in new ways. At the Bar Gaya, which later became Le Boeuf sur le Toit, people chatted, drank and quarrelled the night away. Jean Cocteau was rehearsing his next ballet, a wild farce entitled *Les Mariés de la tour Eiffel,* with music by Darius Milhaud, Georges Auric and Francis Poulenc and costumes by Jean Hugo. As often happens, the war had changed women's appearances. Like Gabrielle Chanel, they had cut their hair, shortened their dresses and now even smoked in public. Often they worked professionally, sometimes even in jobs that had formerly been occupied exclusively by men. A delicate and ancient balance of power was now shifting.

Lo and behold, at the start of this year, a year after the death of Boy Capel, Gabrielle began a new relationship. She had met Grand Duke Dmitri Pavlovich of Russia in Biarritz, where the Russian community liked to summer. In the land he had left behind – the destruction of whose magic in the hell of the Revolution he continually lamented – people were obsessed with perfume. And in the feminine armoury, wasn't perfume the ultimate weapon without which everything else was futile? 'You've got to be able to lead them by the nose,'[7] Gabrielle advised her peers. You seduce a man by sight, you keep him by smell – this was the life lesson she had learned. It was a neat encapsulation of the power that a perfume confers on the woman who wears it.

So there was to be a perfume, but a perfume that was different from all those that had come before. It would have to harmonize with Chanel's vision of fashion and femininity. It would have to be the logical continuation of her creative path. She was an active woman who refused to be dependent on men; after her early success, she had even repaid Boy Capel every last centime of his money, much to his disbelief. Neither a misfit whom nobody wanted to marry for fear of a mismatch, nor a housewife with a dull future decided in advance, Gabrielle Chanel was an independent woman, convinced that freedom could only be achieved through work.

The novelist Colette, another icon of female emancipation who shared the forename Gabrielle, described the couturière as 'a little black bull'.[8] Diaghilev famously urged Cocteau: 'Amaze me!' Accordingly, Gabrielle Chanel never lost her ability to amaze. Just as she had revolutionized fashion, she was about to revolutionize perfume. Obsessed with the idea of being unlike anyone else, she created a perfume in her own unique image. As she perceptively told Paul Morand: 'I wonder why I embarked upon this profession, and why I'm thought of as a revolutionary figure? It was not in order to create what I liked, but rather so as to make what I disliked unfashionable. I have used my talent like an explosive.'[9]

GRAND DUKE DMITRI PAVLOVICH OF RUSSIA

(1891–1942)

1

A cousin of Tsar Nicholas II, Dmitri Pavlovich lost his mother when he was just six days old. His father remarried and had three more children, including Natalia Pavlovna Paley, who went on to marry the couturier Lucien Lelong. Young Dmitri and his sister Maria were brought up in an apartment in the Kremlin by their uncle, the Governor of Moscow. A handsome man, Dmitri was a great success both with women, often older than himself, and with men. On the night of 29–30 December 1916, he was involved in the assassination of Rasputin orchestrated by Prince Yusupov. As a punishment, the tsar exiled him to the Persian front, which ended up saving his life since the rest of the imperial family was eventually tracked down and executed by revolutionaries.

From Tehran, Dmitri went to London, then to Paris. There he was reunited with his sister Maria, whom he later introduced to Gabrielle Chanel. Gabrielle was eleven

1. Grand Duke Dmitri Pavlovitch of Russia, 1913.
2. Dmitri, 1915.

2

years older than him, but they nonetheless became lovers early in 1921. It was probably during their tour of the Riviera that Gabrielle first met Ernest Beaux in Cannes. Although Dmitri's romantic relationship with Gabrielle was short, it turned into a lasting friendship and had a great influence on her creative imagination, and thus her designs.

Gabrielle let him stay at Bel Respiro, her villa in Garches. Dmitri often visited the rue Cambon, where several White Russians in exile found employment. In the store, the *vendeuses* and models addressed him as 'cousin'. This Slavic influence also extended to fashion, when Gabrielle decided to add embroidered designs to her collections. The Kitmir embroidery workshop, founded by Grand Duchess Maria Pavlovna, collaborated exclusively with Chanel from 1921 to 1923. This was Chanel's Russian period, in which Gabrielle took inspiration from garments such as the *roubachka* (a belted peasant blouse), fur coats and capes, traditional embroidery and Byzantine jewelry. Through the Romanovs she discovered the beauty of luxury craftsmanship. She would never look back.

Previous pages: Gabrielle Chanel and Dmitri Pavlovitch, 1920.
This page and opposite: Fashion sketches showing designs decorated with embroidery by the Russian Kitmir workshop, 1922.

Chanel 2435.
Tan Jersey 3 piece
27·36

3

HOW TO START A REVOLUTION

BY 1921, GABRIELLE CHANEL HAD ALREADY LIVED SEVERAL LIVES. She was thirty-seven – old enough to know what she wanted. As befitted her closeness to a circle of progressive and talented artists, her instincts always drove her to turn her back on the past. She was fascinated by innovation and her curiosity was always on high alert. She now approached Ernest Beaux, a Moscow-born perfumer whose creations featured a significant use of synthetic ingredients, which had only recently been discovered. Aldehydes give richness and complexity to the tones of a fragrance but with great lightness, and they also add an aesthetic dimension, a sense of sparkle. Beaux viewed his craft with the ambition of an artist, and compared creating a perfume to composing a piece of music, with every element adding its own clear note. Before the Russian Revolution, he had been technical director at Rallet, the largest perfume house in Russia.

The fact that Ernest Beaux had worked in imperial Russia was another point in his favour for Gabrielle, who was just

Previous page: Gabrielle Chanel photographed by Man Ray, *c.* 1935.

beginning her relationship with the exiled Romanov Grand Duke Dmitri Pavlovich. To explain this affinity, she liked to say: 'Inside everyone from the Auvergne, there is an Oriental one doesn't realize is there – the Russians revealed the Orient to me.'[10] Increasingly charmed by the Russians exiled from that fabulous and bountiful empire, she began to recruit them to work at the rue Cambon. Several *vendeuses*, models and seamstresses were hired from the best salons in St Petersburg. Russia was such an inspiration to Gabrielle that she even hired Russian embroiderers and gave them the task of re-creating traditional peasant blouses, yielding one of the numerous aesthetic paradoxes that made up her grammar of style.

That Beaux's employer Rallet had formerly specialized in soaps and other toiletries also appealed to Gabrielle and her obsession with cleanliness. 'I who love woman wanted to give her clothes in which she would be comfortable [...]. I wanted to give her a perfume, but an artificial perfume. I insist on artificiality, just as a dress is artificial, fabricated. I am a dress-making artisan. I don't want rose or lily of the valley; I want a perfume that is a compound.'[11]

What man could have come up with such a brilliant idea? At the heart of the creation of N°5 was the daring idea of combining natural essences with an unprecedented quantity of synthetic aldehydes. In that era, luxury meant smelling of heliotrope, gardenia, jasmine or rose. Several years earlier, on the tricentenary of the founding of the Romanov dynasty, Beaux had created Le Bouquet de Catherine, an early combination of synthetic molecules with natural florals, but it had met with widespread indifference. Perhaps it was ahead of its time. As always, success requires the right product at the right moment.

Every myth needs an origin story. The details of this particular tale often vary, but the essential thread remains the same. The setting is the early spring of 1921, in the neighbourhood of La Bocca in Cannes, where Ernest Beaux had his lab. It was there that Rallet had been relocated by its parent company, Chiris. Twelve miles away lay Grasse, the international capital for the production of raw materials for perfume. Armed with instructions from Gabrielle Chanel, Beaux tried out various combinations, played with test tubes and generally groped in the dark, faced with this unusual brief. It brings to mind Charles Perrault's fairytale 'Donkeyskin', in which the heroine asks her father, the king, to give her a dress all the colours of the sky, believing it to be an impossible request. Nonetheless, Beaux was up to the challenge. He would later recount that he found the top notes of what would become N°5 by recalling the landscapes of northern Europe, 'where the lakes and rivers exhale a scent of extreme freshness'.[12]

Unsurprisingly, the reality was more arduous than the myth. Ernest Beaux, keen to fulfil Gabrielle's remarkable request, initially submitted to his client a perfume so rich that, as they say in the trade, it had no top notes. Aldehydes would offer a solution; indeed, they were probably already present in the early version, but in smaller quantities. The blend had to be adjusted. Beaux was the first to add so many aldehydes to a fragrance. In this respect, the new perfume was a child of its times, an age when technology was booming. Electricity was widespread, the telephone had been invented and air travel was making distance no obstacle. In an era when the world was getting smaller, and explorers were no longer discovering unknown plants, Beaux declared that the future of perfumes would lie primarily in chemistry.

Eventually, Beaux submitted ten samples to Gabrielle. She tried them one after another, compared them, hesitated, then lingered over the fifth sample. 'Yes, that's what I wanted, a perfume such as has never before been made. A woman's perfume with a woman's scent.'[13]

Gabrielle Chanel did not choose the fifth sample; she recognized it. It was herself in fragrance form. This perfume did not resemble anything that had come before – only her. What did she detect? Aldehyde, neroli and bergamot were the notes that hit her first, as soon as the stopper was removed. The middle notes, which create the signature scent, combined ylang-ylang, jasmine, May roses and iris. Finally, the base notes, those that allow the perfume to last for up to two days, combine vetiver, sandalwood and vanilla. It is no surprise that these unexpected combinations immediately won her over: the fragrance's style is defined by opposites, poised midway between clean and heady. Jacques Polge, the third 'nose' of Chanel, rightly said that N°5 was 'an elusive perfume'.[14]

Beaux did, however, raise the issue of the high cost of this sample. Gabrielle wanted the most costly ingredients. That meant jasmine. 'In that case add more of it. I want to create the most expensive perfume in the world.'[15] Perfume means luxury, she often said throughout her life. In her impoverished youth, her only regret had been the inability to buy it for herself. More so than jewelry or expensive gowns, for her it was the embodiment of opulence. 'A perfume ought to punch you. You don't expect me to sniff for three days, do you, to see if it smells or not? It has to have body, and what gives a perfume body is the most expensive thing there is.'[16] First imported to the Grasse region in the 16th century, jasmine swathes this sunny landscape with a unique scent; it gives off an odour of elegance.

A revolution in fragrance, this perfume did not smell of rose, or vetiver or jasmine: it smelled of something else. Its indescribable and indefinable bouquet immediately distinguished it from its competitors. Gabrielle Chanel, with the help of Beaux, achieved the prodigious feat of re-creating the scent of a woman. It was a fragrance as abstract as the art of its era. And like a work of art, N°5 deserves to be called a masterpiece.

Above and overleaf: Dada-inspired collages celebrating the launch of N°5 perfume, probably dated 1921, mixed media, wood, paper, cotton wool, pins, needles, string, amadou cork. The intended purpose of these compositions (advertising, shop window display, just for fun) is unclear. The set was later given to Serge Lifar by Gabrielle Chanel.

5
CINQ
PARFUM
MYSTERE

5
CINQ
CHANEL
5

ERNEST BEAUX

(1881–1961)

Ernest Beaux joined the Rallet perfume house in Moscow, run by his older brother, in 1898. Awarded the status of suppliers to the Russian imperial court in 1855, the business had recently been acquired by Chiris, a Grasse-based company that specialized in fragrances and medicinal products. It was there that Beaux, hired as a lab technician, learned the craft of soapmaking and perfumery under the guidance of the technical director. This apprenticeship took place at a time of great advances in organic chemistry.

Beaux created his first perfume in 1907, called Royal Rallet, but it was in 1912 that he found success with an eau de cologne named Le Bouquet de Napoléon, launched to celebrate the centenary of the Battle of Borodino. In contrast, his Le Bouquet de Catherine received a far more muted reception in 1913.

Drafted into the army in 1914, Beaux successfully served as a sub-lieutenant in the artillery. He led a number of missions in Russia, and in 1917 joined the intelligence services of the French military in Kiev. His knowledge of the country and its language enabled him to aid in the repatriation of the Allied forces. He was then assigned to the British expeditionary corps in Russia's far north. His courageous conduct on the Russian front earned him the Croix de Guerre and the Légion d'Honneur, as well as a British distinction, the Military Cross, and a Russian one, the Cross of Saint Vladimir. Demobbed in 1919, he later settled in Cannes, where Chiris had relocated its Rallet subsidiary.

1

1. Moscow, *c.* 1870.
2. Russian advertisement for Rallet strawberry milk.
3. The perfumer Ernest Beaux, *c.* 1915.
4. Map of the White Sea, where Beaux served during the First World War.
5. The Rallet factory in the La Bocca neighbourhood of Cannes, which made N°5 perfume from 1921 to 1924.

OCÉAN GLACIAL
Cap Kanin
Péninsule Kanin
Golfe Tcheskaïa
Golfe de Mézen
le Corridor (Détroit)
Mezen
SAMOYEDES
Pinega
CARTE
DE LA
MER BLANCHE

4

Земляничное
Молоко
отъ
загара
Товарищество
высшей парфюмерiи
А. Ралле и Ко.
поставщики
Высочайшаго Двора

2

3

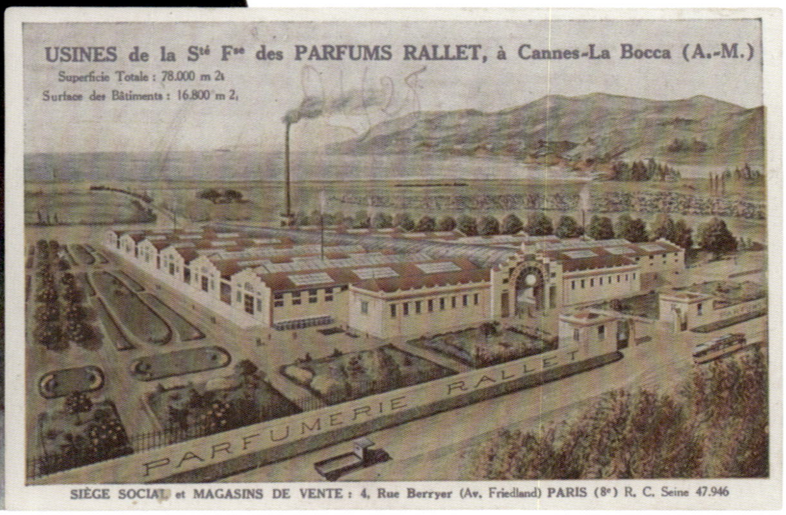

USINES de la Sté Fse des PARFUMS RALLET, à Cannes-La Bocca (A.-M.)
Superficie Totale : 78.000 m 2
Surface des Bâtiments : 16.800 m 2
PARFUMERIE RALLET
SIÈGE SOCIAL et MAGASINS DE VENTE : 4, Rue Berryer (Av. Friedland) PARIS (8e) R. C. Seine 47.946

5

1

It was Beaux to whom Gabrielle Chanel turned when she first set her mind on creating a perfume. His Russian origins, as well as his experience in the manufacture of toiletries, were particularly appealing to this demanding client. After launching N°5 with Gabrielle, Beaux was behind the formulation of all perfumes for Chanel until 1954 and was employed by its subsidiary Parfums Chanel from its founding in 1924. In the post-war period, he became a leading figure in the perfume industry, and gave lectures on the subject that are still considered authoritative. In 1954, Henri Robert, the Grasse-born chief perfumer for Coty, succeeded him as the 'nose' of Parfums Chanel. To date, there have only been four occupants of this role: Henri Robert was followed by Jacques Polge in 1978, then by Olivier Polge in 2013.

2

3

1. Grasse, the global capital of the perfume industry, where Ernest Beaux obtained the raw materials for N°5; his lab was located in the nearby town of Cannes.
2. Jasmine-harvesting in Grasse.
3. A perfume worker, Grasse.

4

5

7

6

4. Fields of flowers, Grasse.
5. A workshop where roses were sorted to make perfume, Grasse region, *c.* 1900.
6. Lab equipment used in the production and purification of essential oils, Grasse, 1936.
7. Vats of essential oils, Grasse, 1931.

*

The origin story then acquired an additional chapter – and by no means the least important. A name had to be found for the chosen sample. 'I present my collection [...] on the fifth day in May, the fifth month of the year, so let's keep the number of the sample, and the number 5 will bring good luck,' Gabrielle Chanel is said to have declared. This response, which has now become legendary in the history of perfume, may have its origins in the artistic zeitgeist of the time. Francis Picabia made playful use of the number 5 in his Dada paintings. Issue number 5 of *L'Esprit nouveau*, Le Corbusier's journal, had just been published. Igor Stravinsky wrote a piece entitled *Les cinq doigts* – 'The Five Fingers'. Another influence was Boy Capel, who passed on to Gabrielle his love of the esoteric, especially the symbolism of the number 5, including the five types of vision in Buddhism or the five-headed gods of Hinduism. The fifth constellation was Leo, Gabrielle's own star sign because of her August birthday. Humans have five senses. The number 5 also recalls the fifth element or quintessence, and thus a symbol of perfection. But most of all, Gabrielle believed in luck, and in her own luck. As a regular at the races with Étienne Balsan, she had often shouted 'Bet on number 5!' – which was, in effect, what she told Ernest Beaux.

'Not a name – a number',[17] she insisted. This was more than a whim: it was a stroke of genius. Thanks to this semantic revolution, Gabrielle Chanel would find a name that worked in all languages, a name that would make all the poetic names that had prevailed until this point look outdated: Après l'Ondée (Guerlain, 1906). Fruit Défendu and Sa Chambre (Poiret, 1918), N'aimez Que Moi (Caron, 1916), Ambre de Delhi (Coty, 1919).

That very evening, Gabrielle Chanel and Ernest Beaux celebrated their discovery in the biggest restaurant in Cannes. Gabrielle placed a spray bottle on the table to judge the effect of her perfume. Every time a woman passed close to the table, she would slow down, sniffing the air, intrigued and perhaps already won over. The couturière immediately knew that she had won her bet.

'Women wear the perfumes they're given as presents. You ought to wear your own, the one you like.'[18] That was the great lesson that Gabrielle Chanel taught her clients. The first person that a woman wants to seduce, and ought to, is herself. Gabrielle would truly love no one after Boy, of whom she said: 'He was the great stroke of luck in my life [...]; he shaped me, he knew how to develop what was unique in me, at the cost of everything else.'[19] The sweet indifference of Dmitri could never make her forget her Pygmalion. N°5 was above all a perfume that could reconcile a woman with herself.

N°5
CHANEL
PARIS

*

'If I were ever to sell a perfume,' said Gabrielle Chanel early in her career, 'it would be so that a woman could perfume herself. I would like to sell the perfume on its own and not the bottle. I would put everything into the perfume, nothing into the presentation.'[20] 'The bottle doesn't matter, so long as it gets you drunk,' says a French proverb. This is precisely what Gabrielle decided. This costly elixir, with the golden colour of a finely aged cognac, would be presented in the plainest of bottles. It would be an aesthetic revolution.

The container for N°5 (since it had to have one) would therefore be just as avant-garde as its contents. With her instinctive aversion towards what had been done before, Gabrielle Chanel turned her back on the era that saw the rise of Art Nouveau, based on masses of curving lines and opulent flowers, like those featured in the Paris Metro stations designed in 1900 by Hector Guimard, and which had seen glass craftsmen competing to create the most lavish and ornamented bottles. So what if all people wanted was curves? Instead, she would offer straight lines and right angles.

She made the radical choice of a square block with sharp corners, whose visual identity owed as much to Russian abstraction as to the German Bauhaus. In 1915, the painter Kazimir Malevich, in a quest for the ultimate in simplification, had exhibited a black square on a white background. The N°5 bottle is a miracle of elegance that succeeds in creating an unlikely synthesis of French-style classicism and modernity. Once again,

Previous pages: The first N°5 bottle, 1921; Gabrielle Chanel, 1935.

it is an example of Gabrielle Chanel's love of unexpected juxtapositions: a very costly product in a minimalist container. 'I have spent my life simplifying things,'[21] she liked to say.

Was the bottle sketched out by Gabrielle herself in Beaux's laboratory in Grasse? Was it born from her memories of Boy Capel's vanity set? As often happens, nobody wants to be responsible for a failure but everyone wants credit for a success. This unusually austere block-like bottle confronted the imagination with a new system of signs: luxury had now become a thing that cannot be seen. Moreover, to underline the fact that a page was being turned, Gabrielle ordered her bottles from the Brosse glassworks, an industrial supplier in the Rouen region.

The very first bottle from 1921, preserved by the Chanel Heritage department, is a striking sight: one might call it a laboratory flask. The stopper is small and square, barely there, and features for the very first time a logo that would become iconic: the double C inside a circle.

Although it was not until 1924 that N°5 found its definitive container, the Chanel fundamentals were already there. There can be no question: the 1921 version is present in the 1924 version. The square stopper became octagonal. Some said this shape was inspired by the Place Vendôme, the location of Gabrielle's beloved Ritz – another unverifiable myth. Most notably, the sharp corners were turned into bevels, their edges filed down to make the bottle less breakable. Three years after its first creation, the N°5 bottle, neater in its proportions, found its perfect formal balance.

As an added refinement, the neck of the bottle was coated with a thin layer of rubber, wrapped with a double row of cotton cord and finished with a double-sided black wax seal. This elegant final touch, applied by hand, brought the perfume even closer to the world of haute couture. Although no longer strictly essential because the modern bottle is so tightly sealed, this artisan finish nevertheless still serves a purpose: it symbolizes luxury.

At any evening event, Gabrielle Chanel remarked, a woman dressed in black outshines all the others. She turned this observation into a rule for life, insisting on black for couture and black and white for perfumery. Once again, this design choice was very much of a piece with her past: the awning of her boutique in Biarritz was white, punctuated with the name Chanel in black lettering, while at her home in Garches, she had all the shutters painted black, to the outrage of her neighbours. The N°5 label would therefore bear its creator's colours. Black and white were indelibly linked with Gabrielle Chanel. She was born in Saumur, the heartland of horse racing, and if N°5 had been a horse belonging to a racing stable, its jockey would surely have worn white silks with a black cap.

As for the monogram, the double C inside a circle, which appeared on the cap of the bottle in 1921 and which is still the Chanel logo, its potential sources are seemingly endless. The initials of 'Coco Chanel' herself? Those of Gabrielle Chanel and the late Boy Capel standing close together but back to back, like an impossible marriage? A memory of the twisting tracery of the stained-glass windows at the Abbaye d'Aubazine? A tribute to the double C used by Queen Catherine de' Medici? So many possibilities compete for attention yet do not rule each other out.

Monograms have their origin in royal seals: they were symbols of power. From the 19th century onwards, their use spread to bourgeois families who, in an attempt to emulate the aristocracy, had their silverware and crockery marked with their initials. Young ladies embroidered linen for their trousseaux with the initials of the two families that were about to be joined. The monogram was therefore fundamental to Gabrielle, as both a mark of ownership and an assertion of her own unique nature. As a final touch, it was enclosed inside a circle, the symbol of perfection.

Regarded in the light of recent semiological research, the monogram reveals even more layers.[22] There is five times as much filled space in the double C logo as negative space: a curious coincidence that creates a definitive link between pure geometry and Gabrielle Chanel's lucky number. The same study has shown that the circle that surrounds the monogram is the echo of a global symbol. More specifically, it can be claimed that throughout history, the circle has always represented the heavens, while the square represents the Earth. A contradiction incarnate, the square bottle is marked by a monogram surrounded by a perfect circle; in this coming together, the heavens finally meet the Earth and mind meets matter so neatly that, ultimately, opposites attract.

The white label also recalled the tracts published by the Dada movement in the same period. And last but not least, the name 'Chanel' was printed in black sans-serif capitals just below the perfume's name. It was the first instance of a couture house branding its products in such a visible and systematic way. Gabrielle imprinted her signature on her work, just as a writer's name appears on the cover of a book, right next to the title.

As for the packaging, in the style of a Cubist collage, it was a simple white-card box with black edging. Its austere lines recalled a death notice, a relevant link in the eyes of a woman who, despite her later loves, would always carry a torch for Boy.

1921

The N°5 bottle and stopper from 1921, seen from various angles.

Chanel lipstick, adorned with the ringed double C monogram (seen from above), 1947–50.

*

There is clearly more than one close connection between Chanel couture and Chanel perfume: they could be called members of the same family. The neat lines of the silhouette, the braided trim of the suits and the starkness of the black and white can all be found in the packaging of N°5. Olivier Polge, the fourth 'nose' of Chanel, quite rightly said that N°5 was 'the style guide for Parfums Chanel'.[23]

N°5 is more than a perfume: it's a concept. Its name is synonymous with refinement, restraint, elegance. By means of its unique positioning, the perfume reflected the artistic personality of its creator and laid out a manifesto for a new kind of luxury. 'That's what luxury is. It isn't the opposite of poverty, it's the opposite of vulgarity,'[24] insisted Gabrielle, who was skilled in the art of combining costume jewelry and precious gems. A glance at the first catalogue for Parfums Chanel is enough to convince anyone: a perfume must be expensive because it is aimed at an elite clientele, to whom the question of price is secondary. 'Invention is the seed, it's the germ. [...] For the plant to grow, you need the right temperature; that temperature is luxury.'[25] Right from the start, Gabrielle Chanel found the ideal climate.

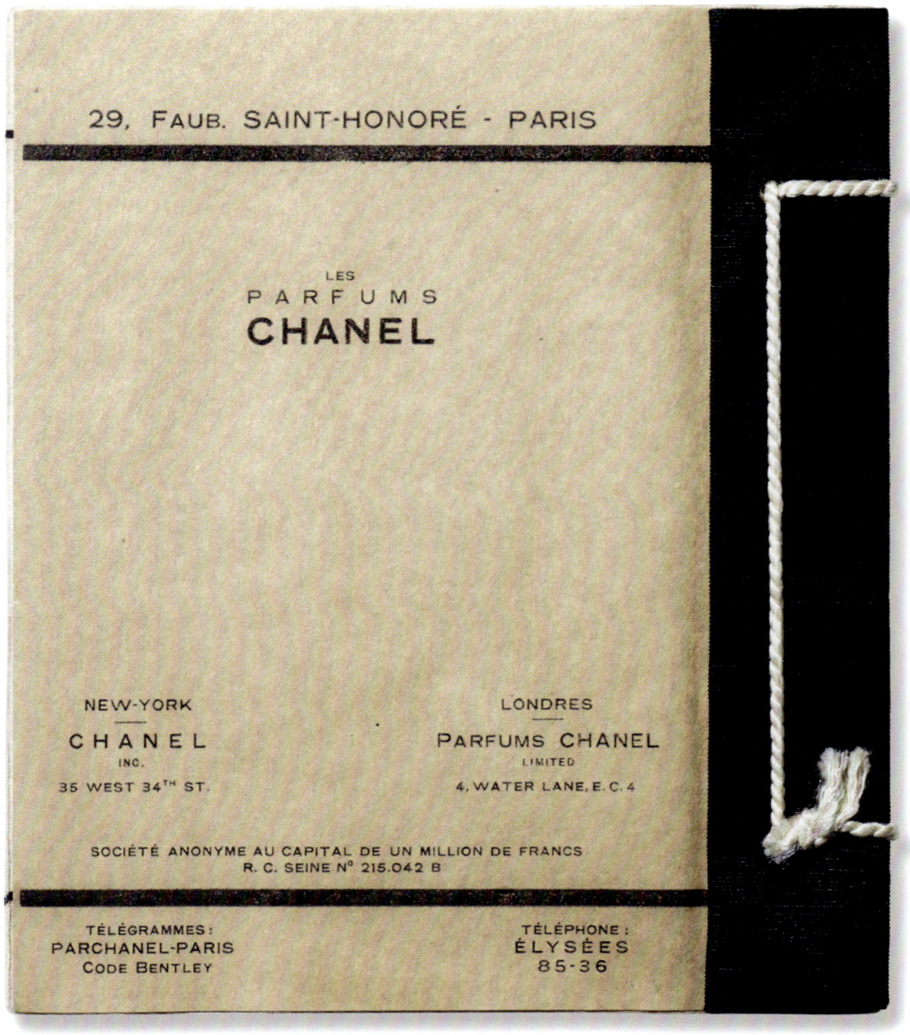

Front and back cover of the first Parfums Chanel catalogue, 1924.

LES PARFUMS CHANEL

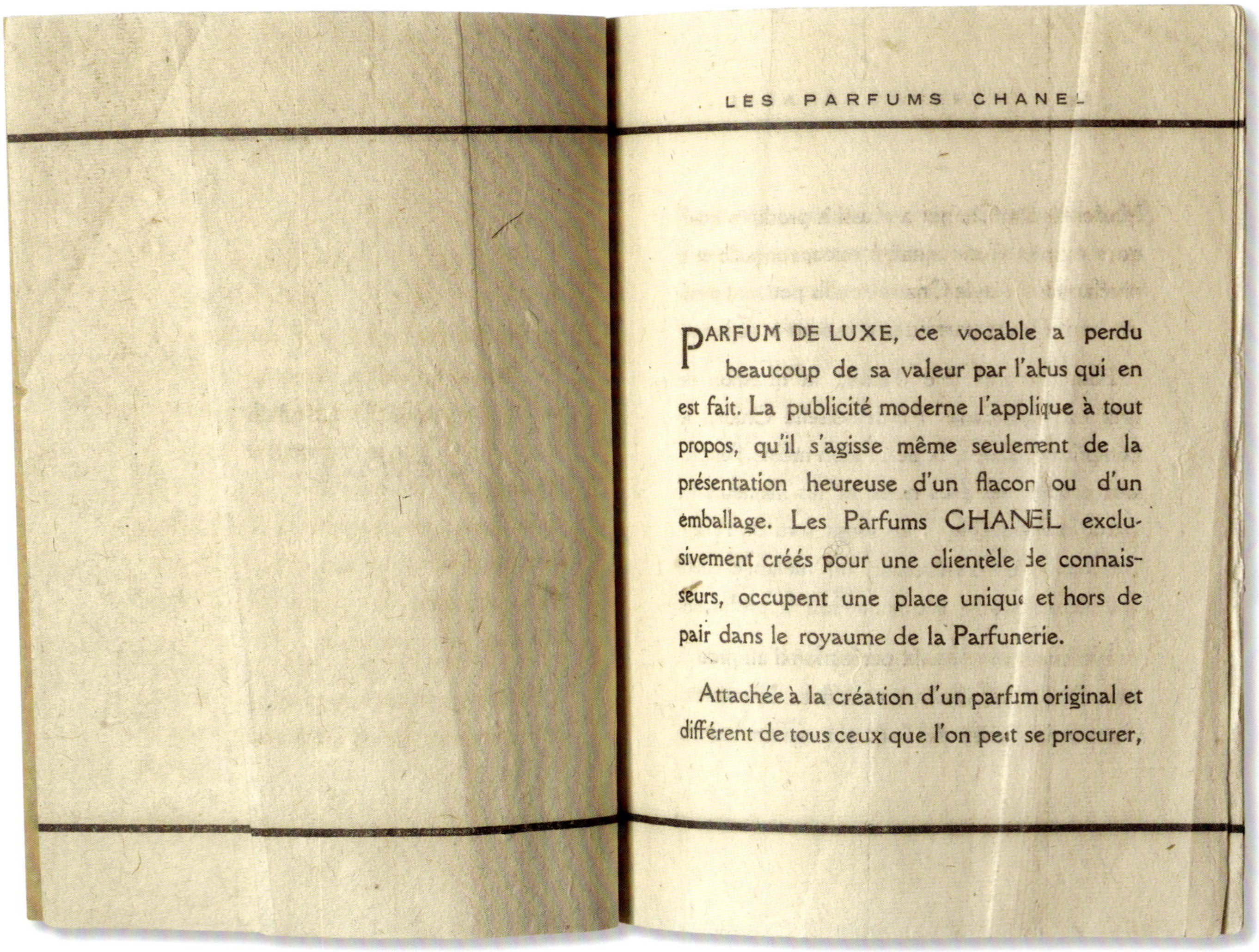

LES PARFUMS CHANEL

PARFUM DE LUXE, ce vocable a perdu beaucoup de sa valeur par l'abus qui en est fait. La publicité moderne l'applique à tout propos, qu'il s'agisse même seulement de la présentation heureuse d'un flacon ou d'un emballage. Les Parfums CHANEL exclusivement créés pour une clientèle de connaisseurs, occupent une place unique et hors de pair dans le royaume de la Parfumerie.

Attachée à la création d'un parfum original et différent de tous ceux que l'on peut se procurer,

Introduction to the first Parfums Chanel catalogue explaining Gabrielle Chanel's strategy, 1924.

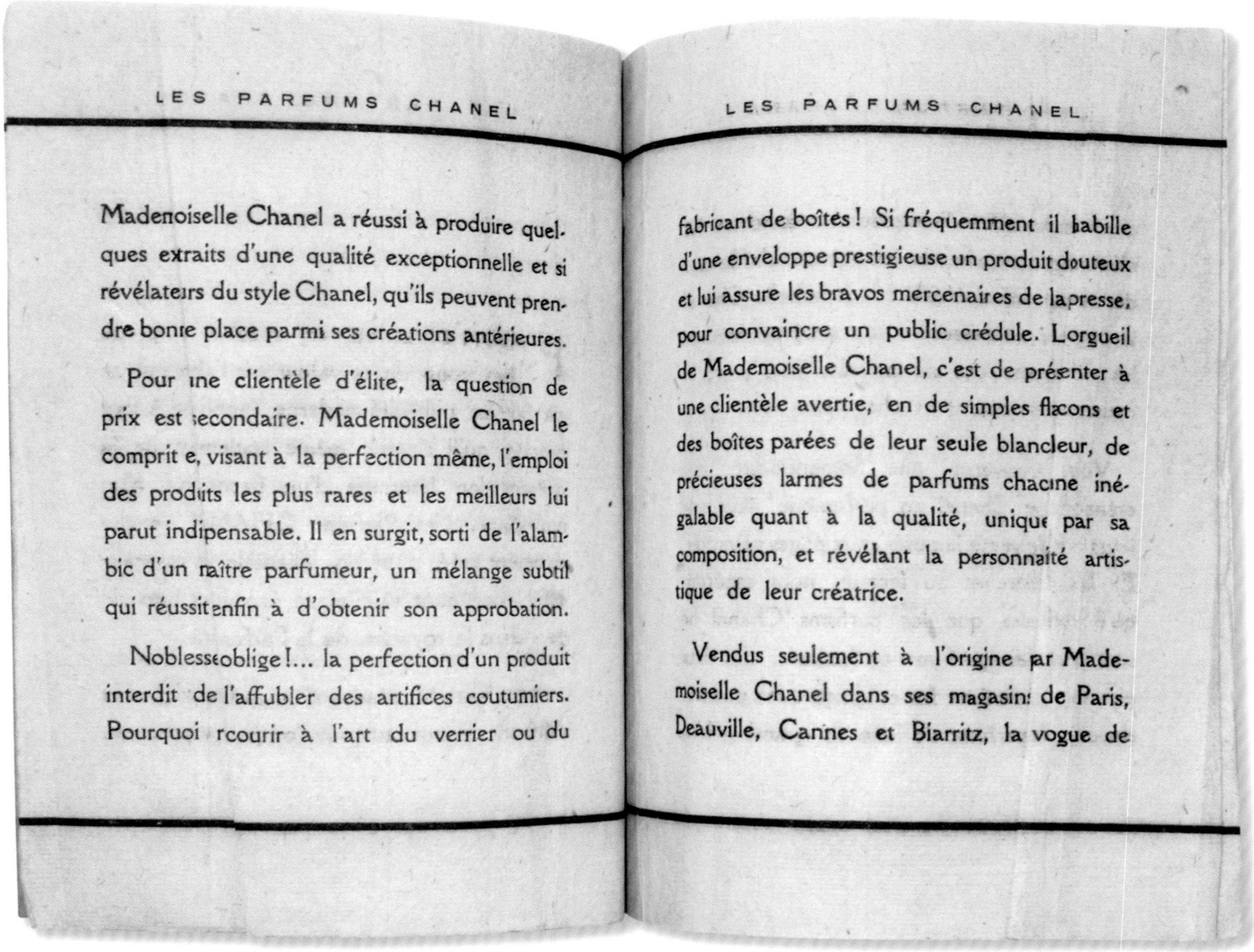

LES PARFUMS CHANEL

Mademoiselle Chanel a réussi à produire quelques extraits d'une qualité exceptionnelle et si révélateurs du style Chanel, qu'ils peuvent prendre bonne place parmi ses créations antérieures.

Pour une clientèle d'élite, la question de prix est secondaire. Mademoiselle Chanel le comprit et, visant à la perfection même, l'emploi des produits les plus rares et les meilleurs lui parut indipensable. Il en surgit, sorti de l'alambic d'un maître parfumeur, un mélange subtil qui réussit enfin à d'obtenir son approbation.

Noblesse oblige !... la perfection d'un produit interdit de l'affubler des artifices coutumiers. Pourquoi recourir à l'art du verrier ou du

LES PARFUMS CHANEL

fabricant de boîtes ! Si fréquemment il habille d'une enveloppe prestigieuse un produit douteux et lui assure les bravos mercenaires de la presse, pour convaincre un public crédule. L'orgueil de Mademoiselle Chanel, c'est de présenter à une clientèle avertie, en de simples flacons et des boîtes parées de leur seule blancheur, de précieuses larmes de parfums chacune inégalable quant à la qualité, unique par sa composition, et révélant la personnalité artistique de leur créatrice.

Vendus seulement à l'origine par Mademoiselle Chanel dans ses magasins de Paris, Deauville, Cannes et Biarritz, la vogue de

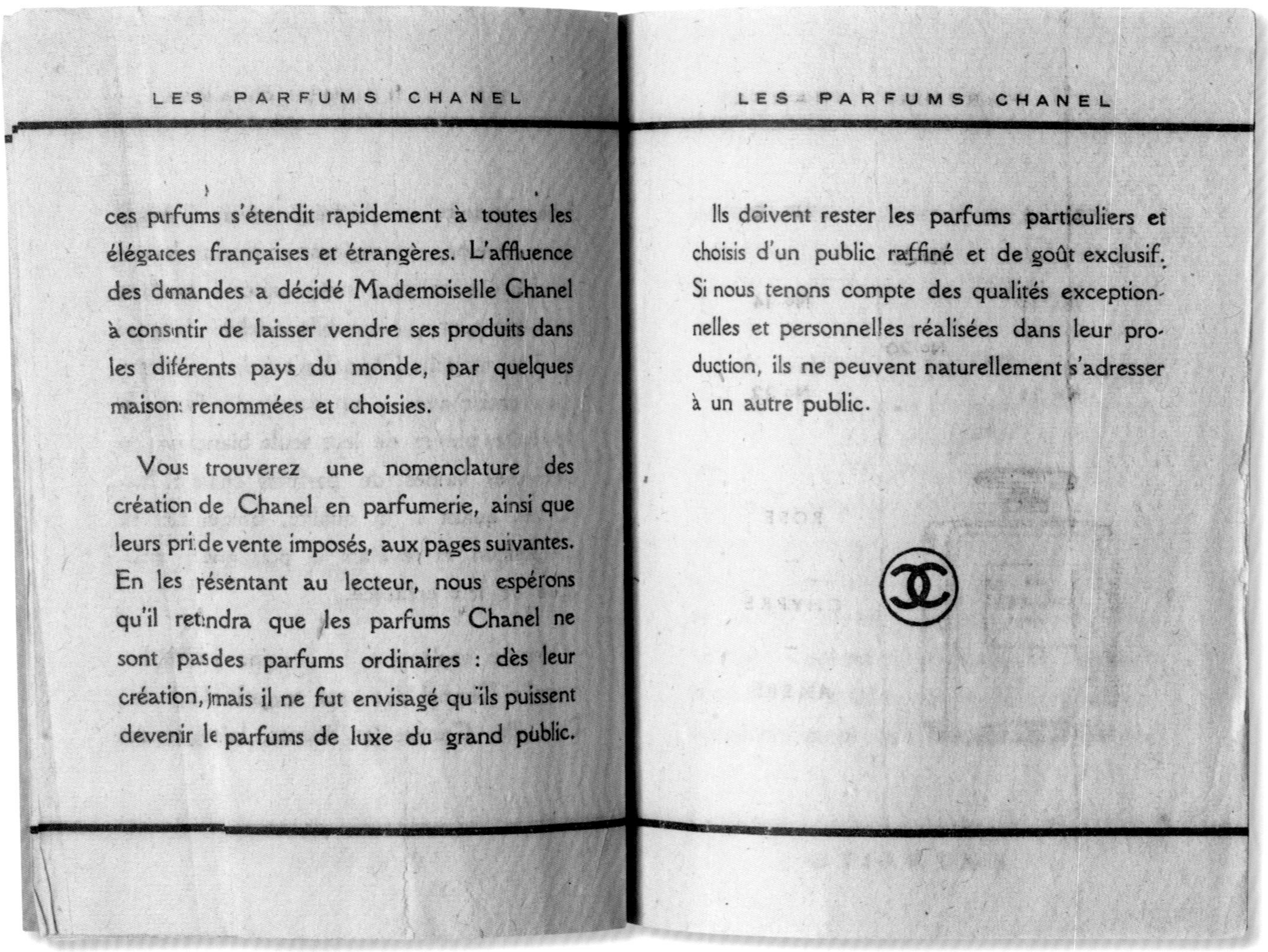

LES PARFUMS CHANEL

ces parfums s'étendit rapidement à toutes les élégances françaises et étrangères. L'affluence des demandes a décidé Mademoiselle Chanel à consentir de laisser vendre ses produits dans les diférents pays du monde, par quelques maisons renommées et choisies.

Vous trouverez une nomenclature des création de Chanel en parfumerie, ainsi que leurs prix de vente imposés, aux pages suivantes. En les présentant au lecteur, nous espérons qu'il retiendra que les parfums Chanel ne sont pas des parfums ordinaires : dès leur création, jamais il ne fut envisagé qu'ils puissent devenir les parfums de luxe du grand public.

LES PARFUMS CHANEL

Ils doivent rester les parfums particuliers et choisis d'un public raffiné et de goût exclusif. Si nous tenons compte des qualités exceptionnelles et personnelles réalisées dans leur production, ils ne peuvent naturellement s'adresser à un autre public.

1924

1

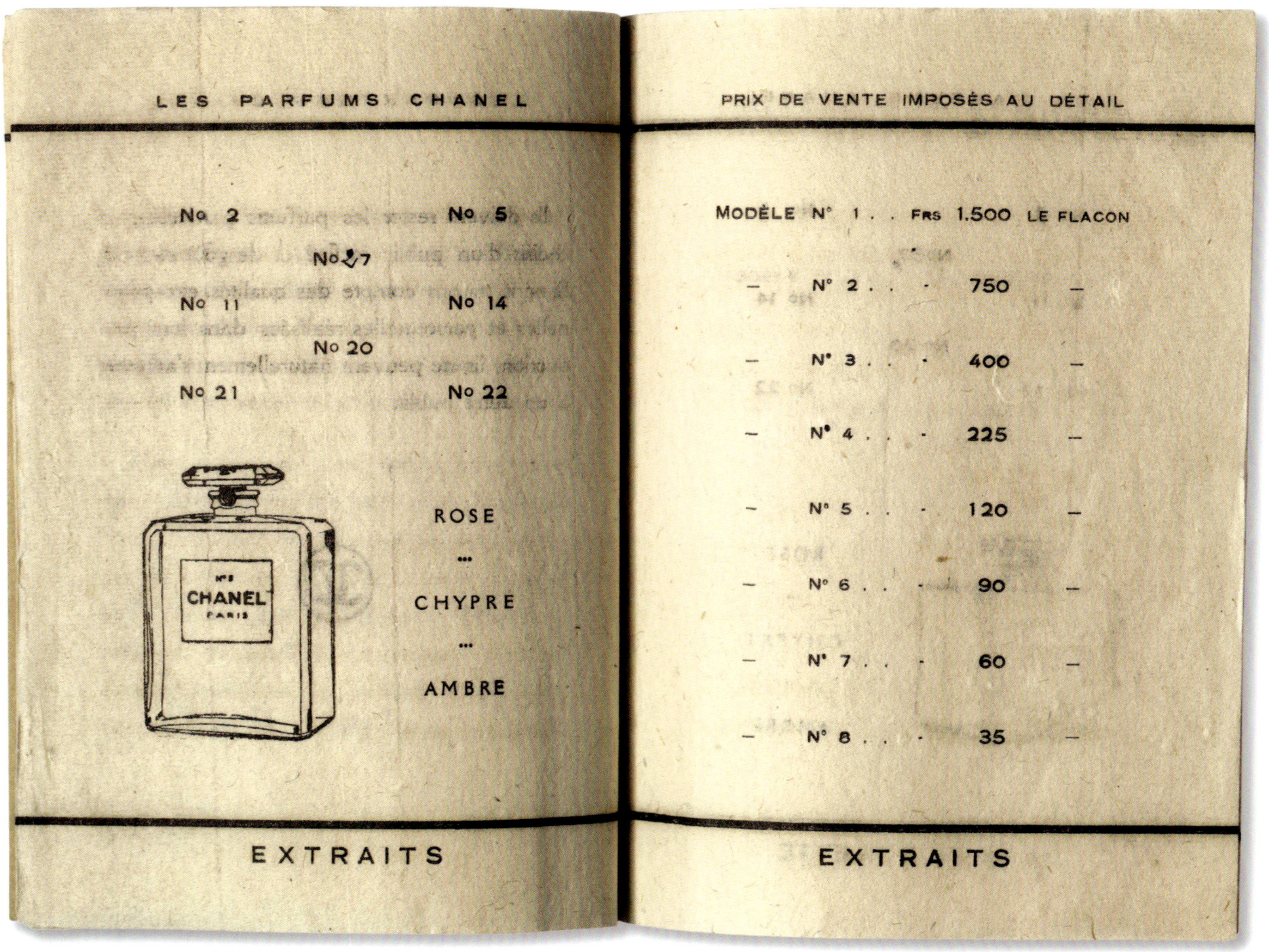

LES PARFUMS CHANEL

No 2 No 5
No 7
No 11 No 14
No 20
No 21 No 22

ROSE
...
CHYPRE
...
AMBRE

EXTRAITS

PRIX DE VENTE IMPOSÉS AU DÉTAIL

MODÈLE	N° 1 . .	FRS 1.500	LE FLACON
—	N° 2 . .	750	—
—	N° 3 . .	400	—
—	N° 4 . .	225	—
—	N° 5 . .	120	—
—	N° 6 . .	90	—
—	N° 7 . .	60	—
—	N° 8 . .	35	—

EXTRAITS

2

1. Bottle and box for N°5, 1924.
2. Double page from the first Parfums Chanel catalogue, with list of fragrances, 1924.

Bottles for N°5 perfume and eau de cologne, 1930s.

1

2

3

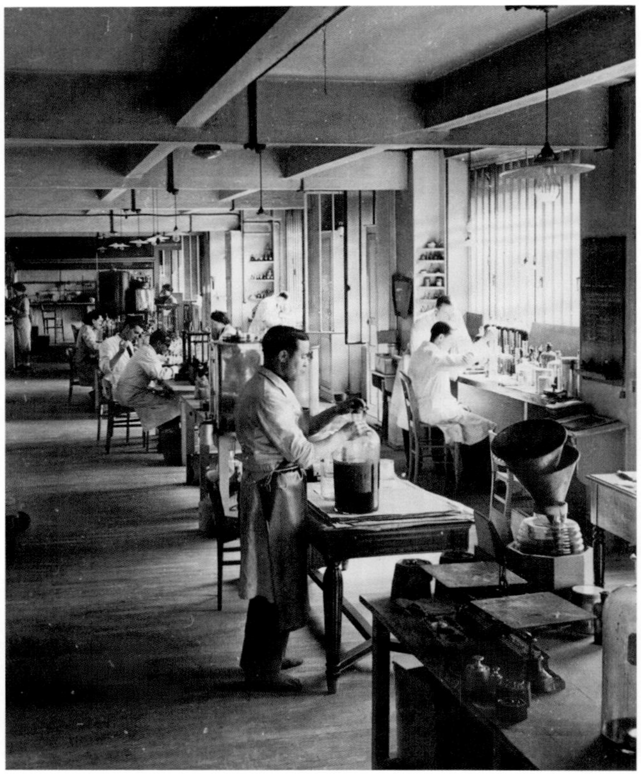

4

5

1. Shelves of perfume concentrates, Chanel factory, Pantin, 1942–43.
2. Technicians in the perfume lab, Chanel factory, Pantin, 1942–43.
3. A perfume technician and manager testing perfumes, Chanel factory, Pantin, 1942–43.
4. Technicians testing perfumes, Chanel factory, Pantin, 1942–43.
5. Technician distilling a concentrate, Chanel factory, Pantin, 1942–43.

6

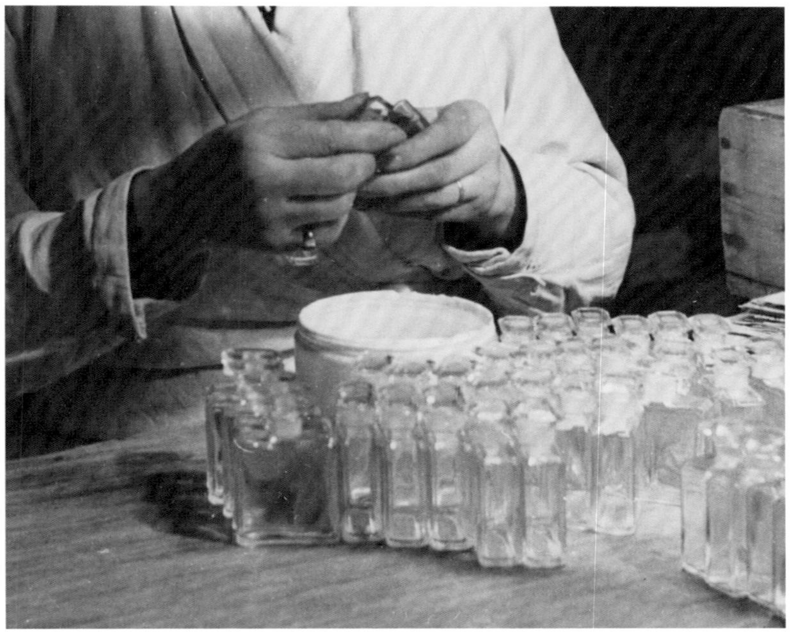

7

8

9

10

6. Sealing a bottle of N°5, Chanel factory, Pantin, 1942–43.
7. Quality checks on the N°5 bottles, Chanel factory, Pantin, 1942–43.
8. The N°5 packaging workshop, Chanel factory, Pantin, 1942–43.
9. The stopper of a N°5 bottle, 1924.
10. Bottles being filled with N°5, Chanel factory, Pantin, 1942–43.

N°5 box and bottle, 1924.

N°5
CHANEL
PARIS

4

A WINNING NUMBER

GABRIELLE CHANEL WAS A GENIUS IN A DISCIPLINE FOR WHICH A NAME HAD NOT YET BEEN INVENTED: MARKETING. When she returned from the Riviera, she brought with her hundreds of bottles of N°5 to give as gifts to her best clients. This consummate liar, who had once invented for herself a father who had gone to make his fortune in America, would confidentially comment to the clients who already loved the scent that had been sprayed in the fitting rooms: 'Oh, yes, the little bottle I gave you the day before yesterday. You want to buy some? You mustn't think of it. Anyway, I don't have any. I don't sell perfumes, my dear. I just happened to stumble upon it in Grasse, in a little perfume shop whose name I don't even remember. I just thought it would make an original gift for my friends.'[26] Unsurprisingly, the gift was soon transformed into a business, and demand continued to grow. The phenomenon also piqued the interest of the press. Gabrielle was interviewed by a fashion writer and discussed her perfume philosophy: 'Spray yourself wherever you might be kissed.'[27] It couldn't be made any clearer: perfume was the weapon of feminine seduction.

Previous page: Gabrielle Chanel, 1931.

Illustration for N°5 by Sem (Georges Goursat), 1921.

The first of Gabrielle Chanel's followers to pay homage to the modernity of N°5 may have been the caricaturist Sem. Although he nicknamed Ernest Beaux 'the minister of the nose', his admiration for Gabrielle continued to grow. In one of his prints, a typical woman of the Roaring Twenties, with close-cropped hair and a drop-waisted gown, gazes up at a bottle of the perfume as if it were a heavenly apparition. This was N°5 as a social phenomenon. Years later, the literary theorist Roland Barthes would write that it had branded the headier scents of its competitors with 'the shameful mark of the out-of-fashion'.[28]

In February 1923, Baron de Meyer photographed and interviewed Gabrielle Chanel for *Harper's Bazaar*.[29] This article, a real accolade because of the fame of her interviewer, allowed her to make a name for herself in the USA.

For the first three years, N°5 was sold exclusively in Chanel boutiques, of which there were four (Paris, Deauville, Cannes and Biarritz). In the flagship store on the rue Cambon, couture was located on the upper floor, while the ground floor was devoted to trinkets, bags and perfume. In a sense, it was perhaps the first concept store, since Chanel sold all the components of the female arsenal there.

Sales of N°5 continued to soar and the Chanel boutiques could no longer satisfy demand. Although this was not a problem for Gabrielle, who wanted her perfume to be reserved for the chosen few, Théophile Bader, the owner of the Galeries Lafayette department store chain, could smell its huge commercial potential and suggested adding the perfume to his shelves. This meant increasing production capacity, since that of Ernest Beaux's lab was limited. Bader introduced Gabrielle to Pierre Wertheimer, whose father Ernest, an industrialist from Alsace, had acquired half of the company Bourjois in 1898. The meeting took place at the Deauville racecourse, where everyone was aware of the success of Épinard, a thoroughbred stallion from the Wertheimer stables. Pierre and his brother Paul had turned a firm that had formerly specialized in theatrical face-paints into a prosperous perfume and cosmetics house. In 1913, an American branch opened, the first stage in an international expansion. Gabrielle set up in business with the Wertheimer brothers. The Société des Parfums Chanel was founded, with the Wertheimers holding 70% of the capital, leaving 20% to Théophile Bader, their intermediary, and 10% to Chanel herself.

The production of Chanel perfumes and cosmetics at the Wertheimers' factory in Pantin, north of Paris, began in 1924. By this time, N°5 was available in three different concentrations. The pure perfume had lost its monopoly and the range had begun to expand, with an eau de cologne and an eau de toilette appearing in the same year. The advent of the spray bottle – a symbol of modernity and convenience – in 1927 allowed the clientele to expand. Despite its high price (the smallest bottle was equivalent to ten hours of a worker's salary), the perfume was ever more in demand. Thanks to the Bourjois distribution network, N°5 quickly became famous all over the world. Britain was conquered in 1924 and the USA also became a major market: branches opened in London and New York in the same year. Soon the whole world was under its spell. N°5 could even be found in Tokyo. The points of sale were primarily department stores, but also smaller perfumeries. By 1929, N°5 was the bestselling perfume in the world.

In March 1931, Gabrielle Chanel set foot on American soil for the first time, accompanied by the faithful Misia Sert, three assistants, fifteen trunks, thirty-five bags and two models. She stayed over in New York before travelling to the West Coast. In front of delighted journalists, she was introduced to Greta Garbo – a meeting of two queens. Hollywood movie stars had long worn Chanel around town, but now, for the first time, Gabrielle herself went to work in cinema, the industry that was her mirror image – an extraordinary technology that had revolutionized image-making just as she had revolutionized fashion. The producer Samuel Goldwyn commissioned her to design costumes for Gloria Swanson for the romantic comedy *Tonight or Never*. As someone who always had her ear to the ground for the latest wonders of the modern world, Gabrielle accepted without hesitation. 'It is through cinema that fashion can now be set,' she declared to the press.[30] In the film, the star of silent movies sported a Chanel wardrobe, restrained in the extreme; a bottle of N°5 was even slipped onto the set, as if to flaunt Chanel's concept of allure.

Nevertheless, Hollywood would never be Gabrielle's territory. After this initial one-off experiment, she preferred to work in France. As always, her instinct led her to work with the best: Jean Renoir (*La Règle du jeu*, 1939) and Luchino Visconti ('The Job', a tale from the anthology *Boccaccio 70*, 1962).

1

2

1. Gabrielle Chanel with her dog Gigot at La Pausa, her villa in Roquebrune-Cap-Martin, *c.* 1930.
2. Gabrielle Chanel on Roussy Sert's yacht near the Lido beach in Venice, 1936.

1

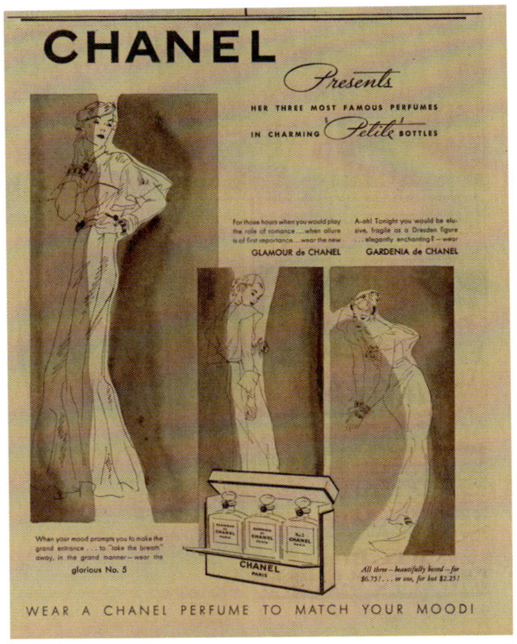

2

3

4

1. Advertisement for N°5 published in the *New York Times*, 1934.
2. Chanel advertisement published in the *New York Times*, 25 November 1934.
3. Chanel advertisement published in the *New York Times*, December 1934.
4. Chanel advertisement published in the *New York Times*, 20 December 1936.

Chanel advertisement published in *Vogue*, 1 November 1936.

Chanel advertisement published in *Vogue*, 1 November 1938.

Chanel advertisement (with photograph by Martin Munkácsi) published in *Harper's Bazaar*, 1 April 1942.

1

2

3

4

*

It is rare for an artist to be able to predict which of their works will best stand the test of time. Gabrielle Chanel was no exception to this rule. She never imagined that N°5 would be such a success, which explains her small stake in the Société des Parfums Chanel. After this first brainchild, other new creations emerged from the mind of Gabrielle Chanel in collaboration with Ernest Beaux. Thus were born N°22 (1922), Gardénia (1925), Cuir de Russie (1927), and Bois des Îles (1928). But none of them would match the phenomenal success of N°5. In 1924, she also launched her first makeup collection, including lipstick, powder and eyeshadow, followed in 1927 by her skincare line.

5

1. Cuir de Russie perfume, 1930s.
2. N°22 perfume, 1920s.
3. Gardénia perfume, *c.* 1925.
4. Bottle and citron-wood box for Bois des Îles perfume, 1928.
5. Chanel N°5 gift set, including a bottle of perfume, a bottle of eau de cologne, N°5 scented powder and a lipstick, *c.* 1938.

Women wear the perfumes they're
given as presents.

You ought to wear your own,
the one you like.

If I leave a jacket behind somewhere,
they know it's mine.

When I was young, the first thing
I'd have done if I'd had any money
would have been to buy some perfume.

I'd been given Floris's Sweet Peas –

I thought it was lovely,
country girl that I was.

Then I realized it
didn't suit me.

Gabrielle Chanel

Gabrielle Chanel photographed by Cecil Beaton, 1937.

1

2

3

4

1. Advertisement for N°5 published in newspapers and international fashion magazines, 1947.
2. Advertisement for N°5 published in *Vogue*, 1 April 1939.
3. Advertisement for N°5 published in *Vogue*, 1 March 1940.
4. Advertisement for N°5 published in *Plaisir de France*, 1946.

Advertisement for N°5 published in *Stage*, February 1937.

5

A LONE RIDER

IN ITS EARLY YEARS, CHANEL ADVERTISEMENTS ALWAYS FEATURED ANONYMOUS MODELS. BUT IN 1937, GABRIELLE CHANEL WAS PHOTOGRAPHED BY FRANÇOIS KOLLAR FOR *HARPER'S BAZAAR*.[31]

With this standing portrait, she became the first brand ambassador for N°5. Leaning against the mantelpiece in her suite at the Ritz, dressed in an evening gown, she was already over fifty but looked ten years younger. It barely mattered, however, since she was the ambassador of modernity – the incarnation not only of a product, but of a way of life. Perfume was a vital ingredient, 'like the soft music that underlies the playing of a love scene,' said Gabrielle.

As a lover of paradoxes, she probably enjoyed the fact that the child of a family from Auvergne had become the epitome of Parisian chic. From that day forth, Gabrielle became 'Mademoiselle Chanel', the most French of names. 'Mademoiselle', like the great actresses who retained that form of address throughout their lives, even if they were wives and mothers. 'Mademoiselle', because the Duke of Westminster had not married a woman who could not give him an heir; because Pierre Reverdy had gone into seclusion at the Abbaye de Solesmes; and because Paul Iribe had been struck down by a heart attack during a holiday at La Pausa, Gabrielle's villa in Roquebrune-Cap-Martin. 'Mademoiselle', forever.

A muse, a communications strategist and a public relations executive: Gabrielle performed all those roles for the perfume

Previous page: Gabrielle Chanel in her apartment at the Ritz, on the Place Vendôme, photographed by François Kollar, 1937.

Advertisement for N°5 published in *Harper's Bazaar*, featuring for the first and last time Gabrielle Chanel in her apartment at the Ritz, 1937.

that over the years would surpass all the rest. Her clothes and her homes were regularly sprayed with N°5. Notified in advance by the doorman at the Ritz, a young assistant would always spray the entrance to the boutique just before Gabrielle arrived. On the rue Cambon, the fragrance wafting up the stairs announced her arrival to her white-smocked staff. Ultimately, she was not just the creator of N°5, she *was* N°5. 'If you love N°5, then do as I do – be faithful to it in all things,' she said in one interview.[32]

Always closely connected with the artists of her age, Gabrielle first met the painter Salvador Dalí in 1929. When the Spanish Civil War was raging, Gabrielle lent him La Pausa, where he stayed with his wife, Gala, who had formerly been married to Paul Éluard. It was there amid the olive trees that Dalí drafted the first chapters of his autobiography. His drawing *Chanel Grand Central Powder Room* (1937), which shows a mysterious shadow approaching a naked female torso in front of a Chanel building, and the post-war photograph in which his famous moustache is pasted onto a bottle of N°5: were these tributes, a form of affectionate teasing, or simply one of his many crazy whims? Influences can always go both ways: just as Gabrielle Chanel was closely connected to the avant-garde of her age, so N°5 served as a source of inspiration for artists – and would continue to do so.

The year 1937 marked a new stage. Chanel's advertising began a lasting shift. Until this point, the perfume had always been associated with couture: 'Both are Chanel,' said the advertisements, showing the bottle alongside a model dressed in Chanel. From this point on, N°5 would be distinct from its creator's garments, as it broke free from fashion like a young bird learning to fly with its own wings. For the first time in France, advertisements showed a bottle of N°5 filling an entire page; it had become autonomous, and thus iconic.

The war confirmed this change: N°5 no longer needed gowns as sidekicks. The couture house was closed by Gabrielle Chanel in 1939 when France mobilized for war, despite the protests of the Chambre Syndicale de la Couture Parisienne, for whom its reputation was a key part of Paris's prestige. 'It is no longer time to make gowns or to dress women whose menfolk are going to be killed,' the couturière declared.[33] But the perfume business carried on. In New York, where Pierre Wertheimer sought refuge in August 1940, carrying in his luggage the formula for N°5, he continued making and marketing the fragrance. Paradoxically, throughout the conflict, this luxury product was sold at the same cooperatives that provided cigarettes and chewing gum to GIs. It was a triumph. For the first time, and without compromising on its quality, N°5 became a mass-market fragrance.

When Paris was liberated, American soldiers stood in line on the rue Cambon to buy bottles of N°5 for the fiancées, wives and mothers whom they would soon see again. In these still-troubled times, the French Forces of the Interior arrived to question Gabrielle about her relationship with a German officer, but she was released after a brief interrogation. She did not reopen her couture house until 1954. As for the Wertheimers, they had cleverly preserved their interests, including Les Parfums Chanel, by placing them in the hands of a figurehead during the war.

1

2

3

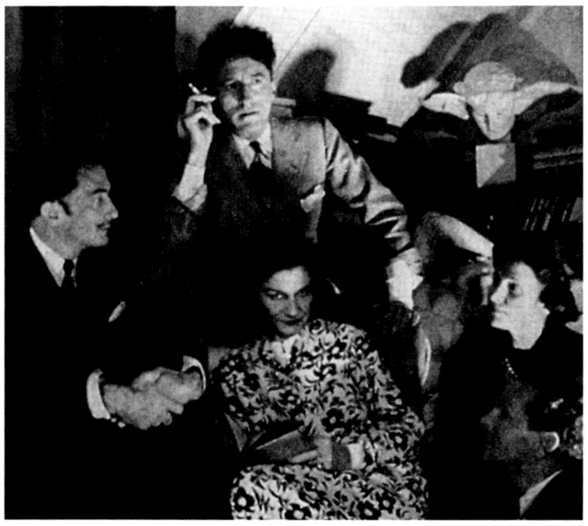

4

5

1. Salvador Dalí, *Chanel Grand Central Powder Room*, pencil and Indian ink on paper, *c.* 1937.
2. Salvador Dalí and Gabrielle Chanel, 1938.
3. Salvador Dalí at La Pausa, Gabrielle Chanel's villa in Roquebrune-Cap-Martin.
4. Gabrielle Chanel surrounded by Salvador Dalí, Jean Cocteau, Gala Dalí and Mr Samossa, in her suite at the Ritz, 1939.
5. Salvador Dalí, Gabrielle Chanel and Georges Auric at a dinner given by the Prince de Faucigny-Lucinge, June 1938.

Salvador Dalí and Philippe Halsman, *The Essence of Dalí*, a photograph of a N°5 bottle decorated with a portrait of Dalí, 1954.

A LONE RIDER

1

2

1. Gift box with purse-sized bottle of N°5, 1930s.

3

2, 3. Gabrielle Chanel with Mr and Mrs François Hugo, Mrs James Field and Pierre Colle, in the courtyard olive tree at La Pausa, her villa in Roquebrune-Cap-Martin, 1938.

1

2

1, 4. American soldiers waiting for the Chanel boutique on the rue Cambon to open, *c.* 1945.
2. Chanel advertisement published in French newspapers, late 1930s.
3. Chanel advertisement published in *L'Officiel de la couture et de la mode de Paris*, March–April 1946.

CHANEL

PARFUMS CHANEL
N° 5
CHANEL
PARIS

3

CHANEL
CHANEL
MILITARY POLICE
S-S 787P
HQ 14

4

*

If Gabrielle Chanel had worked only in fashion, her success might have been fleeting. But she did much more: she foresaw something that would never go out of style. Over the years, N°5 became legendary. Did she unwittingly discover the essence of timeless femininity? A line written by Cocteau for *Les Mariés de la tour Eiffel* in 1921, just as the perfume was being born, could be read as a premonition: 'Since these mysteries are beyond me, let us pretend that we are the ones responsible for them.'

N°5, 1921 and 1924.

Gabrielle Chanel at work, 1937.

NOTES

NOTES ON THE MAIN TEXT

1 Paul Morand, *The Allure of Chanel* (1976), trans. Euan Cameron, London: Pushkin Press, 2013, p. 78.
2 Quoted in Edmonde Charles-Roux, *Chanel: Her Life, Her World, and the Woman Behind the Legend She Herself Created*, New York: Knopf, 1975, p. 208.
3 'Voici Chanel 59', *Elle*, 9 February 1959, p. 22.
4 Paul Morand, *The Allure of Chanel*, p. 6.
5 Edmonde Charles-Roux, *Chanel: Her Life, Her World, and the Woman Behind the Legend*, London: Jonathan Cape, 1976, p. 109.
6 Henri Robert, quoted in Élisabeth de Feydeau, *Les parfums, histoire, anthologie, dictionnaire*, Paris: Robert Laffont, Bouquins, 2011, pp. 583–85.
7 Justine Picardie, *Coco Chanel: The Legend and The Life*, London: HarperCollins, 2010.
8 Colette, 'Chanel par Colette', *Bravo*, April 1930, p. 36.
9 Paul Morand, *The Allure of Chanel*, p. 175.
10 Ibid., p. 93.
11 Pierre Galante, *Mademoiselle Chanel*, Chicago: Henry Regnery, 1973, pp. 67–68.
12 Ernest Beaux, 'Souvenirs d'un parfumeur', *Industrie de la parfumerie*, Paris: Presses Documentaires, October 1946, vol. 1, no. 7, p. 230.
13 Pierre Galante, *Mademoiselle Chanel*, p. 74.
14 Jacques Polge in conversation with the author, 2020.
15 Pierre Galante, *Mademoiselle Chanel*, p. 74.
16 Claude Delay, *Chanel solitaire*, London: Collins, 1973, p. 86.
17 Cited by Élisabeth de Feydeau, *Les parfums, histoire, anthologie, dictionnaire*, Paris: Robert Laffont, Bouquins, 2011, p. 583.
18 Cited by Claude Delay, *Chanel solitaire*, p. 28.
19 Paul Morand, *The Allure of Chanel*, p. 36.
20 Cited by Sophie Chassard, 'Le Numéro 5 s'expose au Palais de Tokyo', *Le Monde*, 7 May 2013.
21 Interview featured in the documentary by Jean Lauritano, *Les guerres de Coco Chanel*, Slow Production / INA – Institut National de l'Audiovisuel / Arte France, 2019.
22 Odilon Cabat and Patrice Civanyan, 'Sémiologie du Monogramme CHANEL', 2020.
23 Olivier Polge in conversation with the author, 2020.
24 'Chanel parle Chanel', *Elle*, 28 August 1964, p. 58.
25 Paul Morand, *The Allure of Chanel*, p. 169.
26 Pierre Galante, *Mademoiselle Chanel*, p. 76.

27 Pierre Galante, *Mademoiselle Chanel*, p. 77.
28 Roland Barthes, *Système de la mode*, Paris: Seuil, 1967, p. 167.
29 Baron de Meyer, 'Mlle Chanel tells Baron de Meyer her opinions on good taste', *Harper's Bazaar*, February 1923, pp. 29–30, 96.
30 Emma Cabire, 'Le cinéma et la mode', *La Revue du cinéma*, 1 September 1931, p. 21.
31 *Harper's Bazaar*, October 1937, pp. 93–93, 100–01, 113.
32 Alice Chavanne, 'Chanel, celle qui a inventé la femme d'aujourd'hui', *Elle*, 23 May 1955, pp. 64–65.
33 Isabelle Fiemeyer, *Chanel intime*, Paris: Flammarion, 2011, p. 169.

NOTES ON THE BIOGRAPHIES

I Élisabeth de Gramont, *La treizième heure*, Paris: Grasset, 1935; repr. 2020, p. 154.
II Marie-Dominique Lelièvre, *Chanel and Co*, Paris: Denoël, 2013, p. 81.
III Paul Morand, *The Allure of Chanel* (1976), trans. Euan Cameron, London: Pushkin Press, 2013, p. 48.
IV Claude Arnaud, quoted in Isabelle Cahn, Guy Cogeval and Marie Robert, *Misia, reine de Paris*, exhibition catalogue, Paris: Gallimard/Musée d'Orsay, 2012.
V Arthur Gold and Robert Fizdale, *Misia: The Life of Misia Sert*, New York: Morrow Quill Paperbacks, 1981, p. 302.
VI Paul Morand, *Venises*, Paris: Gallimard, 1971; repr. 1983, p. 93.
VII Interview in *La Gazette des Arts*, 10 February 1923.
VIII Pierre Galante, *Les Années Chanel*, Paris: Mercure de France/Paris Match 1972, p. 103.

PICTURE CREDITS

2–3 Horst P. Horst / Conde Nast via Getty Images
4–5 Bibliothèque nationale de France
6–7 © CHANEL
13 © Sasha / Hulton Archive / Getty Images
18.1 Martinie / Roger Viollet via Getty Images
18.2 Collection Igor Stravinsky, Fondation Paul Sacher, Basel
18.3 Bettmann / Getty Images. © ADAGP / DACS / Comité Cocteau, Paris 2021
18.4 Bettmann / Getty Images
18.5 Album / Alamy Stock Photo
19.6 Martinie / Roger Viollet via Getty Images
18.7 © Collection Mr Ferréol de NEXON
19.8 Bridgeman Images
19.9 Apic / Getty Images
20.1 © CHANEL – Archives familiales / All Rights Reserved.
21.2 Album / Alamy Stock Photo
22.1 Apic / Getty Images
23.2 © CHANEL – Archives familiales / All Rights Reserved.
24.1 All Rights Reserved.
24.2 © Comœdia Illustré, 1910. Photo Félix / All Rights Reserved.
24.3 © CHANEL – Archives familiales / All Rights Reserved.
25.4 © CHANEL – Archives familiales / All Rights Reserved.
25.5 Bibliothèque nationale de France / Vogue Paris
27.2 Fine Art Images / Heritage Images / Getty Images
28.1 The Trustees of the British Museum
28.2 Archives Charmet / Bridgeman Images
28.3 © Private collection
29.4 Collection Igor Stravinsky, Fondation Paul Sacher, Basel
29.5 Bridgeman Images. © Succession Picasso / DACS, London 2021
29.6 © Private collection
30.1 Bridgeman Images. © Succession Picasso / DACS, London 2021
30.2 © Succession Picasso / DACS, London 2021
30.3 Bettmann / Getty Images
30.4 Keystone-France / Gamma-Keystone via Getty Images
31.5 © Man Ray 2015 Trust / DACS, London 2021
31.6 Hulton-Deutsch Collection / Corbis via Getty Images
31.7 Théâtre de l'Atelier in Le Théâtre et Comœdia Illustré / Diktats bookstore
32.1 CPA Media Pte Ltd / Alamy Stock Photo
33.2 Chronicle / Alamy Stock Photo
34.1 Boris Lipnitzki, Roger-Viollet / Getty Images. Cocteau drawing: © ADAGP / DACS / Comité Cocteau, Paris 2021
34.2 Roger-Viollet / Shutterstock. © ADAGP / DACS / Comité Cocteau, Paris 2021

34.3 © Man Ray 2015 Trust / DACS, London 2021
35.4 Pictorial Press Ltd / Alamy Stock Photo
35.5 Bibliothèque nationale de France / Vogue Paris
35.6 Lebrecht Music Arts / Bridgeman Images. © ADAGP / DACS / Comité Cocteau, Paris 2021
35.7 Lebrecht Music & Arts / Alamy Stock Photo
38.1 © Sem (Georges Goursat)
38.2 © Photo Frères SEEBERGER – Bibliothèque nationale de France
39.3 © Sem (Georges Goursat)
40.1, 2 Bibliothèque nationale de France / Vogue Paris
41.3 Musée national Picasso-Paris / RMN-Grand Palais
43 Boris Lipnitzki, Roger-Viollet / TopFoto
45 © Archives de Paris / Ville de Paris
48.1 Fine Art Images / Diomedia
49.2 Apic / Getty Images
50–51 © CHANEL / All Rights Reserved.
52–53 Courtesy of Fashion Institute of Technology, New York / SUNY FIT Library Special Collections and College Archives
55 © Man Ray Trust / ADAGP Paris 2021
61 © CHANEL
62–63 © CHANEL
64.1 Henry Guttmann / Hulton Archive / Getty Images
65.4 Patrick Guenette / 123RF.com
65.3 Album / Alamy Stock Photo
65.2 Bridgeman Images
65.5 Archives Municipales, Cannes
66.1 Roger-Viollet / TopFoto
66.2 Denis Brihat / Gamma-Rapho via Getty Images
66.3 Alinari / TopFoto
67.4 Keystone-France / Gamma-Keystone via Getty Images
67.5 Boyer / Roger Viollet via Getty Images
67.7 Roger-Viollet / TopFoto
67.6 Photo Centre Pompidou, MNAM-CCI, Dist. RMN-Grand Palais / Philippe Migeat. Photo Pierre Boucher
70 © CHANEL
71 © CHANEL – Archives familiales / All Rights Reserved.
76, 77, 79, 80–81, 82.1, 82.2, 83 © CHANEL
84–85.1, 2, 3, 4, 5, 6, 7, 8, 10 © Jean Roubier
85.9, 86–87 © CHANEL
89 AKG-images
91 © Sem (Georges Goursat)
95.1 © CHANEL – Archives familiales / All Rights Reserved.
95.2 © V.H. Grandpierre / Vogue Paris
96–97, 98 © CHANEL
99 © CHANEL / Courtesy Howard Greenberg Gallery, New York. Estate of Martin Munkácsi
100–101 © CHANEL
103 © The Cecil Beaton Studio Archive
104.1 Hprints.com
104.2, 104.3, 104.4, 106 © CHANEL
107, 109 © CHANEL / Ministère de la Culture – Médiathèque du Patrimoine, Dist. RMN-Grand Palais / François Kollar
112.1 © Salvador Dalí, Fundació Gala-Salvador Dalí, DACS 2021
112.2 Prismatic Pictures / Bridgeman Images
112.3 © Rights to the image of Salvador Dalí reserved. Fundacio Gala-Salvador Dalí, Figueres, 2021 / All Rights Reserved.
112.4 Photo Agneta Fischer. Vogue US / Conde Nast
112.5 Photo Roger Schall © Collection Schall
113 Philippe Halsman / Magnum Photos, © DACS 2021. © Salvador Dalí, Fundació Gala-Salvador Dalí, DACS 2021
114.1 © CHANEL
114.2, 115.3 Photo Roger Schall © Collection Schall
116.1 Robert Doisneau / Gamma-Rapho / Getty Images
116.2, 117.3 © CHANEL
117.4 © CHANEL – photography by Serge Lido
118 © CHANEL
119 Photo Roger Schall © Collection Schall

ACKNOWLEDGMENTS

Olivier Polge and Thomas du Pré de Saint Maur, who currently safeguard – in their own ways – the future of an iconic fragrance, generously shared their knowledge and passion for N° 5 with me. Our fascinating conversations fuelled this book, and I owe them the greatest of thanks.

I would like to express my deep gratitude for the trust, support and willingness shown to me by the team at the Direction du Patrimoine Chanel, especially Hélène Fulgence.

Many thanks to Kitty d'Alessio for her invaluable account of the N° 5 American advertising campaigns, as well as to Jean-Paul Goude and Carole Bouquet for their lively and enlightening memories of collaborating with Chanel.

Olivier Andreotti skilfully matched the images with this text and I am grateful for the warm encouragement he offered me from the start.

My commissioning editor at Thames & Hudson, Adélia Sabatini, orchestrated this collective adventure from London with kindness and professionalism; our collaboration will remain a treasured memory.

Pauline Dreyfus
Paris, March 2021

INDEX

Page numbers in *italic* refer to the illustrations. Page numbers in **bold** refer to the biographies.

This boxed set consists of two volumes which may not be sold separately

First published in the United Kingdom in 2021 by Thames & Hudson Ltd,
181A High Holborn, London WC1V 7QX

Reprinted 2023

Texts by Pauline Dreyfus
Creative direction and design by Olivier Andreotti (Toluca Studio, Paris)

British Library Cataloguing-in-Publication Data
A catalogue record for this book is available from the British Library

ISBN 978-0-500-02312-9

Printed in China, by Artron Art (Group) Co., Ltd.

FSC www.fsc.org MIX Paper from responsible sources FSC™ C019910